"In the Name of Allāh, the Most Beneficent,
the Most Merciful"

Contents

Introduction...   5

Backdrop to Sūrah Jinn...   7

Uniqueness of the holy Qur'ān... 16

Lifespan of Jinns... 18

Man was Created in the Best Stature... 19

Warning to Those who Reject Faith 20

Importance of Listening to the holy Qur'ān Attentively 21

Dismay on the Day of Judgement... 28

Places of Prostration... 34

Intimidating the holy Prophet ﷺ... 34

Everything is in the Hands of Allāh ﷻ... 39

Prophets that Were sent 56

Guarding the Revelation 61

Translation of Jinn ... .… 69

Sūrah Jinn - Verses 1-5.... 70

Sūrah Jinn - Verses 6-10 ... …... 71

Sūrah Jinn - Verses 11-15... 72

Sūrah Jinn - Verses 16-21.... 73

Sūrah Jinn - Verses 22-26 74

Sūrah Jinn - Verses 27-28.... 75

Introduction

All praises are due to Allāh ﷻ. May peace, salutations and blessings be upon our guide and mentor, the final and beloved Prophet Muhammad ﷺ, upon his noble Sahābah ؓ, Tābi'īn and those who follow in their footsteps till the Day of Judgement, Āmīn.

As humans, we are not the only creation on Earth and we are not the only creation who will have to systematically give account for their deeds on the Day of Judgement. Allāh ﷻ created the Jinns which also reside on the Earth. Just as there are Muslims and non-Muslims in the human beings, so too, there are Muslims and non-Muslims amongst the Jinns.

In terms of our actions in this world, Jinns and human beings are on the same footing. Both creations are instructed to believe and worship Allāh ﷻ. Allah ﷻ states in the holy Qur'ān:

وَمَا خَلَقْتُ الْجِنَّ وَالْإِنْسَ إِلَّا لِيَعْبُدُونِ ۞

I have created man and Jinn only to worship Me. (51:56)

In terms of the shar'ī perspective, all scholars mention that the Jinn are classed as intelligent beings, along with human beings and angels.

Indeed, this point of them being held accountable is emphasised by the fact that they are specifically addressed in the Qur'ān and a whole Sūrah has been named after them. Sūrah Jinn elaborates more on this creation, in relation to them accepting Islām during the time of the holy Prophet 器. There is also some mention of their history, in terms of what they used to do before the guidance came to them.

My beloved Shaykh and teacher, Muftī Saiful Islām, has beautifully done a commentary of Sūrah Jinn. This is full of references to the holy Qur'ān and hadīth, exploring and providing insight into this creation which we have little knowledge about. We will find much theories on this creation which are only speculative and baseless. Here, we can be assured that this information is genuine and authentic, knowledge which has been revealed to us by Allāh 器 through the medium of his beloved Prophet 器.

May Allāh 器 reward my Shaykh and bless him in his knowledge and allow us to benefit from him. May Allāh 器 reward all those who assisted in the compilation of this book and make this a means of their salvation on the Day of Judgement, Āmīn.

Zakiya Saeeda
Student of JKN
June 2020

Backdrop to Sūrah Jinn

If there were those that turned away from accepting īmān, then Allāh ﷻ had the power to bring about another nation who would not be like the previous nation, and as this Sūrah continues on from the previous Sūrah, this is the message that resonates. In the previous Sūrah; Sūrah Nūh, Sayyidunā Nūh ﷺ preached to his people for 950 years but despite this great length of time, only about 80 people accepted his message. Those that disbelieved met with the fate of being drowned in the flood.

A new creation is introduced in this Sūrah and this is the creation of the Jinns; a creation which although is invisible to the human eye, like humans, is also going to be held accountable to Allāh ﷻ. The message that resonates as the Sūrah is introduced is that even though there maybe those that reject īmān, there will always be those that will stay steadfast on the truth. This is mentioned in the following verse:

قُلْ أُوحِيَ إِلَيَّ أَنَّهُ اسْتَمَعَ نَفَرٌ مِّنَ الْجِنِّ فَقَالُوٓا إِنَّا سَمِعْنَا قُرْآنًا عَجَبًا ۞

"Say, 'Revelation has come to me that a group of Jinn attentively listened to me (reciting the Qur'ān) and said (to their fellow Jinn when they returned to their places), 'Indeed we have heard a most astounding (wonderful) Qur'ān.'" (72:1)

According to the tafsīr of the Qur'ān, nine Jinn accepted īmān. The circumstances surrounding the revelation were as follows:

The holy Prophet 🕌, after preaching his message in Makkah for a period of ten years with little success, and with the subsequent death of his uncle Abū Tālib, turned his focus to the city of Tā'if in propagating the message to the Thaqīf tribe. He spoke to three brothers; Abd Yalīl, Mas'ūd and Habīb who were the sons of Amr ibn Umayya Ath-Thaqafī and were recognised as the chiefs of Tā'if. Instead of responding with hospitality, they grew even more hostile. The first brother said, "l would tear the robes of the Ka'bah if it is true that you are God's Messenger."

The second brother said, "Has God found no one other than you to be his Messenger?"

The third brother said, "By God, I won't speak to you. If it is true that you are God's Messenger, you are too great for me to speak to you. If, on the other hand you are lying, you are not worth answering."

They did not stop there with their hostility, rather they sent their youngsters to chase him out of the city, pelting him with stones until his blessed feet began to bleed. His faithful servant, Zaid ibn Hārithah who was accompanying him fought hard to protect him from the stones.

The holy Prophet 🕌 then sought refuge in an orchard that belonged to two brothers, Utbah and Shaybah; the sons of Rabī'ah who commanded positions of high esteem in the Quraysh. The holy Prophet

🌸 remained unaware that he was under their watchful eyes and as he sat down he made the following du'ā:

"To You my Lord, I complain of my weakness, lack of support and the humiliation I am made to receive. Most Compassionate and Merciful! You are the Lord of the weak, and you are my Lord. To whom do You leave me? To a distant person who receives me with hostility? Or to an enemy you have given power over me? As long as you are not displeased with me, I do not care what I face. I would however be much happier with Your mercy. I seek refuge in the light of Your face by which all darkness is dispelled and both this life and the life to come are put in their right course against incurring your wrath or being the subject of Your anger. To You I submit until I earn Your pleasure. Everything is powerless without Your support."

Despite the two brothers being opposed to the holy Prophet 🌸, during this particular moment they felt pity for the holy Prophet 🌸. They sent their servant with a platter of grapes to give to the holy Prophet 🌸. Before eating, the holy Prophet 🌸 recited the du'ā, "Bismillāh (In the name of Allāh 🌸)." The servant upon hearing these words looked at him in shock and remarked, "This is something no one says here."

The servant was known as Addās. He was a Christian who was from the town of Nineveh. When he told the holy Prophet 🌸 his name and place of origin, holy Prophet 🌸 remarked, "Then you come from the same place as the noble Prophet Yūnus 🌸." Addās became even more astonished saying, "How do you know about Yūnus, for when I left Nineveh, not even ten people knew about him?" The holy Prophet ﷺ replied, "He was my brother and like me, he was a prophet." Upon hearing this, Addās became overjoyed and started kissing the holy Prophet ﷺ on his head, hands and feet. As the two brothers watched the events that were unfolding from a distance, one of the brothers said to the other brother, "That man has certainly spoilt your slave."

When Addās left the holy Prophet ﷺ, the two asked as to why he had behaved in this manner to which Addās replied, "There can be no one on earth better than him. He has indeed told me something which no one but a prophet would know." The brothers replied, "You should be careful, Addās. He may try to convert you while your religion is better than his."

It was at this time the holy Prophet ﷺ had travelled to the Ukkāz market in Tā'if and after being rejected by the leaders and the common people that this verse was revealed. The holy Prophet ﷺ had then gone to a place called Nakhlah and had been engaged in reciting the holy Qur'ān when the Jinn who were present were attentively listening.

From the time of Sayyidunā Nūh ﷺ, the Jinn used to transcend to the heavens and attempt to overhear the revelation being descended to the prophets. With the coming of the last Prophet, the Jinns were prevented from eavesdropping and they would be pursued by a ball of fire when they did so.

Allāh ﷻ revealed the above verse of Sūrah Jinn. The Jinns, after listening to the recitation of the holy Qur'ān immediately accepted īmān and believed, so this became a turning point for the holy Prophet ﷺ, comforting his heart after the disturbing experience before.

This group consisted of nine Jinns, who went back and spread the message to the other Jinns. This then resulted in a second group of 90 Jinns who came to the holy Prophet ﷺ in accepting the message.

According to the books of history, the incident of the holy Prophet ﷺ preaching to the Jinn occurred six times. Just as the Prophet ﷺ was sent as a mercy for mankind in guiding humans, in the same way he was also sent to guide the Jinns.

Allāh ﷻ says in the Qur'ān:

﴿١٩﴾ أَلَمْ تَرَ أَنَّ اللهَ خَلَقَ السَّمٰوٰتِ وَالْأَرْضَ بِالْحَقِّ ۚ إِنْ يَّشَأْ يُذْهِبْكُمْ وَيَأْتِ بِخَلْقٍ جَدِيْدٍ

﴿٢٠﴾ وَمَا ذٰلِكَ عَلَى اللهِ بِعَزِيْزٍ

"Do you not see that Allāh has created the heavens and the earth with the truth? If He wills, He could remove you and bring a new creation. This is not at all difficult for Allāh." (14:19-20)

Allāh ﷻ articulates in another verse:

وَمَا خَلَقْتُ الْجِنَّ وَالْإِنْسَ إِلَّا لِيَعْبُدُونِ ۞

"I have created man and Jinn only to worship Me." (51:56)

In the Arabic language, any word with the letters Jīm and Nūn has a meaning of concealment. For example:

- Jinn – is a creation of Allāh ﷻ which is hidden from our eyes.
- Jannah – is a garden hidden from our eyes.
- Junūn – is madness which is concealed in a person's mind.
- Janīn – this refers to the foetus which is concealed in the mother's womb.
- Junnah – this refers to a shield which protects a person from their enemies.

There are four unique creations which Allāh ﷻ has created:

Angels – they are created from nūr (light). They obey Allāh's ﷻ every order and have no element of disobedience in them. Even though they have no sins, a human being can achieve a higher status than the angels through obeying Allāh ﷻ. The prophets reached the status higher than that of the angels because of their dedication and perseverance in preaching the message.

Allāh ﷻ says in the holy Qur'ān regarding the angels who are in charge of punishment:

عَلَيْهَا مَلَٰئِكَةٌ غِلَاظٌ شِدَادٌ لَّا يَعْصُونَ اللهَ مَا أَمَرَهُمْ وَيَفْعَلُونَ مَا يُؤْمَرُونَ ۝

"Harsh and strong angels are appointed over it who never disobey what Allāh commands them and who carry out exactly what they are instructed." (66:6)

The Jinn - they were created from smokeless fire as mentioned in the following verse:

وَالْجَآنَّ خَلَقْنَاهُ مِن قَبْلُ مِن نَّارِ السَّمُومِ ۝

"And the Jinn We created before (man) out of fire derived from a scorching wind." (15:27)

There are two categories of Jinns; there are the pious Jinns who are believers and the disobedient Jinns who are known as the Shayātīn.

Human beings – The elements of water, fire, earth and air are present in the different types of creation but the element of earth is more dominant in the creation of man.

Animals – This includes all the different species of creation that we see around us. Animals have been created to assist and be of service to human beings, as well as a delight to the aesthetic senses of the human experience.

The angels and animals will be free from accountability because they have no sense of free will. The Jinns and human beings will face accountability. Those that disobeyed Allāh ﷻ will suffer the punishment of the Hellfire and those that obeyed Allāh ﷻ will be rewarded accordingly.

Iblīs was a Jinn who initially worshipped Allāh ﷻ for hundreds of thousands of years but his pride got the better of him and this led to his ruination, when he refused to bow down to Sayyidunā Ādam ﷷ when Allāh ﷻ commanded him to do so. This led to him being expelled from Jannah and being given the name of Shaytān.

وَإِذْ قُلْنَا لِلْمَلَٰٓئِكَةِ اسْجُدُوا لِآدَمَ فَسَجَدُوا إِلَّا إِبْلِيسَ أَبَىٰ وَاسْتَكْبَرَ وَكَانَ مِنَ الْكَافِرِينَ ۞

"When we told the angels, 'Prostrate to Ādam,' they all prostrated to Ādam except Iblīs. He refused, was arrogant and was from among those who rejected." (2:34)

His mission thus became that of leading mankind astray, despite the fact that he was banished from Jannah because of not bowing down to a human being; whom he felt was beneath him as he was made from fire and Sayyidunā Ādam ﷷ was made from clay.

قَالَ مَا مَنَعَكَ أَلَّا تَسْجُدَ إِذْ أَمَرْتُكَ قَالَ أَنَا خَيْرٌ مِنْهُ خَلَقْتَنِي مِنْ نَارٍ وَخَلَقْتَهُ مِنْ طِينٍ ۞

"He said, 'What stopped you that you could not make sajdah when I commanded you?' He replied, 'I am better than him! You have created me from fire and created him from clay.'"(7:12)

وَأَنَّهُ كَانَ يَقُوْلُ سَفِيْهُنَا عَلَى اللهِ شَطَطًا ۞

"Undoubtedly the ignorant among us (the Jinns) used to say things about Allāh that transgresses the limit (when they attributed partners and children to Allāh)." (72:4)

What was the quality missing in Iblīs that lead to his destruction? He had the three following qualities prior to being expelled from Paradise:

1. He was the greatest ābid (worshipper) as he worshipped Allāh ﷻ for thousands of years. There was not a place that remained where he had not prostrated.
2. He was the greatest ālim (scholar).
3. He was the greatest ārif – he recognised Allāh ﷻ to the extent that when Allāh ﷻ commanded him to leave from Jannah, he knew that Allāh ﷻ would not reject the Du'ās because Allāh ﷻ does not get affected by anger as a human would do. Hence, Shaytān knew that his request would be accepted and not turned down.

However, the quality that was lacking in his character was that he was not an āshiq (possessing love) for Allāh ﷻ. A person who truly loves Allāh ﷻ, after submitting their will to Allāh ﷻ, then whatever Allāh ﷻ commands a person to do, they will carry it out immediately without questioning.

Shaytān using his logic, thought that because he was made of fire and Sayyidunā Ādam عليه السلام was made of clay, then when fire burns it rises up and the earth which Sayyidunā Ādam ﷺ was composed of remains on the ground. Hence, he felt that he was more superior to Sayyidunā Ādam ﷺ. What he failed to realise is that fire is destructive whereas the earth is constructive, and many things are derived from this. The superiority of the earth is not only in the material form but even in the form of being created out of it.

Hence, all the rebellious Jinns follow the Shaytān and are known as Shayātīn.

Uniqueness of the holy Qur'ān

قُلْ لَّئِنِ اجْتَمَعَتِ الْإِنْسُ وَالْجِنُّ عَلَى أَنْ يَّأْتُوْا بِمِثْلِ هٰذَا الْقُرْاٰنِ لَا يَأْتُوْنَ بِمِثْلِه وَلَوْ كَانَ بَعْضُهُمْ لِبَعْضٍ ظَهِيْرًا ۞

"If mankind and the Jinn combined to (try to) produce something similar to this Qur'ān, they would not be able to produce anything like it even if they (act as) assistant (to) each other." (17:88)

أَمْ يَقُوْلُوْنَ تَقَوَّلَهُ ۚ بَلْ لَّا يُؤْمِنُوْنَ ﴿33﴾ فَلْيَأْتُوْا بِحَدِيْثٍ مِّثْلِه إِنْ كَانُوْا صَادِقِيْنَ ﴿34﴾

"Or are they saying, "He has forged it?" The fact of the matter is that they refuse to accept īmān. Let them produce a speech like it if they are truthful." (52: 33-34)

أَمْ يَقُوْلُوْنَ افْتَرَاهُ ۗ قُلْ فَأْتُوْا بِعَشْرِ سُوَرٍ مِّثْلِه مُفْتَرَيَاتٍ وَّادْعُوْا مَنِ اسْتَطَعْتُمْ مِّنْ دُوْنِ اللّٰهِ

إِنْ كُنْتُمْ صَادِقِيْنَ ۝

Or do they say, He (the holy Prophet) has fabricated it. Say, "Produce ten fabricated Sūrahs like any in it and besides Allāh, call whoever you can (to assist you) if you are truthful." (11:13)

The uniqueness of the holy Qur'ān remains unsurpassed that even up until this day, no one has been able to produce even a single verse let alone an entire Sūrah, in measuring up to its standard.

فَإِنْ لَّمْ تَفْعَلُوْا وَلَنْ تَفْعَلُوْا فَاتَّقُوا النَّارَ الَّتِيْ وَقُوْدُهَا النَّاسُ وَالْحِجَارَةُ ۖ أُعِدَّتْ لِلْكَافِرِيْنَ ۝

"If you cannot accomplish the feat, and you will never be able to do so, then fear that Fire, the fuel of which is men and stones. It has been prepared for the disbelievers." (2:24)

In this verse, Allāh ﷻ states that no matter how hard a person might try, they will never be able to produce the like thereof, because not only is the holy Qur'ān a book of guidance but it is our means of salvation if we choose to abide by and follow it. The words in the holy Qur'ān are not just merely elements of speech or writing, but are distinct meaningful expressions, commands and instructions that penetrate the soul in a way no other book has the power to do so, in bringing the soul back to life through its spiritual training and nourishment.

Lifespan of Jinns

Ibnul Jawzī ﷺ narrates in his book 'Sifatus-Safwah' that Sayyidunā Sahl ibn Abdullāh ﷺ once saw a Jinn praying salāh in front of the Ka'bah. Sayyidunā Sahl ibn Abdullāh ﷺ looked intently at him. After the Jinn had finished praying, the Jinn asked him as to why he was gazing at him. Sayyidunā Sahl ibn Abdullāh ﷺ replied that he was fascinated by the beautiful cloak he had on, to which the Jinn replied, "I have been wearing this garment for 700 years. And this is the same garment I had on when I met Sayyidunā Īsā ﷺ. I wore the same garment when I met the holy Prophet ﷺ and I am from the same group of Jinns whom the first verse of Sūrah Jinn was revealed regarding."

Shāh Wali-Ullāh Muhaddith ﷺ narrates in one of his books that he met a Jinn who was a sahabī Jinn. Shāh Wali-Ullāh ﷺ lived 300 years ago which would make the Jinn over 1000 years old. The Jinn are a creation of Allāh ﷻ who have been given a very long lifespan.

When the following verse was revealed:

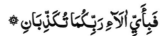

"So, which of the favours of your Lord do the two of you (man and Jinn) deny?" (55:16)

The Jinns upon hearing this verse, immediately replied, "From your blessings not a single thing we deny."

Man was Created in the Best Stature

لَقَدْ خَلَقْنَا الْإِنْسَانَ فِيْ أَحْسَنِ تَقْوِيْمٍ ۞

"Undoubtedly, We created man in the best form." (95:4)

Man has not only been given a good physique but has been given the faculty of the greatest intellect in the kingdom from all creation. His ability to use reason and logic is exclusive to his species alone:

وَلَقَدْ كَرَّمْنَا بَنِيْ أَدَمَ وَحَمَلْنَاهُمْ فِي الْبَرِّ وَالْبَحْرِ وَرَزَقْنَاهُمْ مِّنَ الطَّيِّبَاتِ وَفَضَّلْنَاهُمْ عَلَى كَثِيْرٍ مِّمَّنْ خَلَقْنَا تَفْضِيْلًا ۞

"It is indeed true that We have granted an honour to the children of Ādam. We carried him on land and sea, provided him with pure sustenance and granted him great superiority over many of Our creation." (17:70)

Allāh ﷻ has bestowed creation to be subservient to man. From animals we derive food and nourishment, they carry our loads, from their wool and fur we derive adornment in beautifying and clothing ourselves, and these are just a few examples.

Warning to Those who Reject Faith

وَإِن تَتَوَلَّوْا يَسْتَبْدِلْ قَوْمًا غَيْرَكُمْ ثُمَّ لَا يَكُونُوٓا أَمْثَالَكُم ۝

"If you turn away (from obeying Him), He will substitute you
with another nation who will not be like yourselves." (47:38)

يَٰٓأَيُّهَا ٱلَّذِينَ ءَامَنُوا مَن يَرْتَدَّ مِنكُمْ عَن دِينِهِ فَسَوْفَ يَأْتِي ٱللَّهُ بِقَوْمٍ يُحِبُّهُمْ وَيُحِبُّونَهُۥٓ أَذِلَّةٍ
عَلَى ٱلْمُؤْمِنِينَ أَعِزَّةٍ عَلَى ٱلْكَٰفِرِينَ يُجَٰهِدُونَ فِى سَبِيلِ ٱللَّهِ وَلَا يَخَافُونَ لَوْمَةَ لَآئِمٍ ۚ ذَٰلِكَ
فَضْلُ ٱللَّهِ يُؤْتِيهِ مَن يَشَآءُ ۚ وَٱللَّهُ وَٰسِعٌ عَلِيمٌ ۝

"O you who have īmān! Whoever among you turns away from
his religion then Allāh can soon bring another nation whom He
loves and who loves Him; who will be kind towards the believers, stern towards the disbelievers and who will strive in Allāh's
way without fearing the criticism of those who criticise. This is
the grace of Allāh that He grants to whoever He desires. Allāh is
All-Surrounding, All-Knowing." (5:54)

After the holy Prophet ﷺ had preached for ten years to the people,
only a handful of people became Muslims. Initially, after three years
of receiving the divine revelation, he invited his extended family
members to accept the message but the response was far from wel-
coming, in their hostility and rejection of the message.

After the death of his uncle Abū Ṭālib, he was left without any protection and exposed to the wrath and anger of the Quraysh. In the

same year his beloved wife, Sayyidah Khadījah ﷺ also died. Thus, this year was named, 'The year of grief.'

Importance of Listening to the holy Qur'ān Attentively

وَإِذَا قُرِئَ الْقُرْاٰنُ فَاسْتَمِعُوْا لَهٗ وَاَنْصِتُوْا لَعَلَّكُمْ تُرْحَمُوْنَ ۞

"When the Qur'ān is recited, then listen attentively to it and remain silent so that mercy may be shown to you." (7:204)

When the holy Qur'ān is being recited, there should be complete silence and a person should listen to it; being focused and absorbed in its recitation.

يَّهْدِيْٓ إِلَى الرُّشْدِ فَاٰمَنَّا بِهٖ ۖ وَلَنْ نُّشْرِكَ بِرَبِّنَآ اَحَدًا ۞

"It points towards righteousness so we believed in it and we shall never ascribe any partner to our Lord." (72:2)

The Jinns did not even momentarily halt after listening to the revelation, realising that these were the words of Allāh ﷺ. Immediately it penetrated into their hearts and they accepted īmān. After a lifetime of disobedience, the time had finally arrived where they would stand firm in their decision; they would never go back to committing shirk.

Even amongst the species of Jinns, they follow various different religions. The believing Jinns felt regret at the time that they had wasted in doing things other than Allāh's ﷺ worship in ascribing partners to Him. The following verse below refers to the concept of trinity:

وَأَنَّهُ تَعَالَىٰ جَدُّ رَبِّنَا مَا اتَّخَذَ صَاحِبَةً وَّلَا وَلَدًا ﴿٣﴾ وَأَنَّهُ كَانَ يَقُوْلُ سَفِيْهُنَا عَلَى اللهِ
شَطَطًا ﴿٤﴾

"Most exalted is the majesty of our Lord, Who has neither taken a wife or a child. Undoubtedly, the ignorant among us used to say things about Allāh that transgress the limit." (72:3-4)

Before the advent of Islām, the polytheists used to ascribe power to the Jinns and seek aid and assistance from them. For example, if they had been travelling and nightfall had descended, they would seek refuge in the name of the leader of the Jinn to protect them from all harm being committed from all the Jinns that were under their control. The leader of the Jinns would then increase in their arrogance upon hearing these invocations uttered by human beings.

One such person had supplicated this invocation. Upon falling asleep, he had a dream in which he was attacked by the Jinns who created many difficulties for him. He realised that through reading this invocation he had not benefitted in any way. A Jinn came to him and said, "You are a fool. It is pointless asking refuge from ourselves. Now a prophet has come in Madīnah, if you seek refuge by saying, 'In the name of the Lord of Muhammad from the evil of the foolish people of the tribe,' you will be protected."

The person then asked the Jinn, "Where will I find this prophet?" The Jinn replied, "Beneath the palm trees." The person then went on to find the holy Prophet ﷺ and accepted Islām, thus becoming one of the Companions of the Prophet ﷺ.

Even nowadays, many people seek the help of āmils who claim that they can solve all of a person's problems using the assistance of Jinn. Their false claims almost equate them with God-like qualities. These people use the Jinns to extract information from them. From the pieces of information they will say, although there maybe one or two correct pieces of information, it will contain a greater portion of lies. Imām Bukhārī 🙴 narrates the following hadīth: *Sayyidah Ā'ishah 🙴 reported, some people asked the Prophet 🙵 about soothsayers. The holy Prophet 🙵 said: "They are upon nothing." They said, "O Messenger of Allāh 🙵, sometimes they speak about things which come true." The Prophet 🙵 said, "Those are the words snatched by the Jinn, who whisper it into the ears of their friends and it is mixed with more than one hundred lies."*

$$\text{وَأَنَّا ظَنَنَّا أَن لَّن تَقُولَ الْإِنسُ وَالْجِنُّ عَلَى اللهِ كَذِبًا} ۞$$

"And we always thought that no human or Jinn could ever lie about Allāh." (72:5)

Many people remain gullible and naive, this was also the case amongst the Jinns. They never imagined that any human being or Jinn could be bold enough to lie about Allāh 🙵 and as a consequence, they accepted the practice of shirk assuming it to be correct.

Many times, when the majority of people are doing something wrong, this is used as a reason by many to further indulge in the sin; that somehow, they feel that the effects of the sin is lightened and not as severe since 'everyone is doing it'. We need to look at Islām in a pure and wholesome manner, we should not be influenced by the majority but rather, do those actions that are permitted in Islām and refrain from doing those things which are prohibited.

وَأَنَّهُ كَانَ رِجَالٌ مِّنَ الْإِنسِ يَعُوذُونَ بِرِجَالٍ مِّنَ الْجِنِّ فَزَادُوهُمْ رَهَقًا ۞

"Indeed there were those from mankind who used to seek protection from men of the Jinns and (thereby) increased them (the Jinns) all the more in rebellion." (72:6)

By seeking protection from the leaders of the Jinns from being harmed by other Jinns, the Jinns would have a sense of superiority over the humans, and hence they would feel that they were too great and powerful to submit to Allāh ﷻ.

وَأَنَّهُمْ ظَنُّوا كَمَا ظَنَنتُمْ أَن لَّن يَبْعَثَ اللهُ أَحَدًا ۞

"They (these Jinns) thought as you (the sinners) think that Allāh shall not resurrect anyone." (72:7)

The Jinns also thought that when they die, then this would be the end and because they believed that they would not be resurrected, they failed to mend their ways. Similar to the disbelievers who held the same belief:

وَقَالُوا مَا هِيَ إِلَّا حَيَاتُنَا الدُّنْيَا نَمُوتُ وَنَحْيَا وَمَا يُهْلِكُنَا إِلَّا الدَّهْرُ ۚ وَمَا لَهُم بِذَٰلِكَ مِنْ عِلْمٍ
إِنْ هُمْ إِلَّا يَظُنُّونَ ۞

"They say, 'This is nothing but our worldly life. We live and die

and it is only time that will destroy us." They have no proof for this but only speculate." (45:24)

The Jinns after listening to the verses came to the realisation that this world was a test:

اَلَّذِیۡ خَلَقَ الۡمَوۡتَ وَالۡحَیٰوةَ لِیَبۡلُوَکُمۡ اَیُّکُمۡ اَحۡسَنُ عَمَلًا ؕ وَهُوَ الۡعَزِیۡزُ الۡغَفُوۡرُ ۙ

"He has created death and life to test which of you carry out the best deeds. He is the Mighty, the Most Forgiving." (67:2)

This life is a test and the only way to succeed in this test is by obeying Allāh ﷻ and following His Messenger ﷺ.

وَاَنَّا لَمَسۡنَا السَّمَآءَ فَوَجَدۡنٰهَا مُلِئَتۡ حَرَسًا شَدِیۡدًا وَّشُهُبًا ۙ﴿۸﴾ وَّاَنَّا کُنَّا نَقۡعُدُ مِنۡهَا مَقَاعِدَ لِلسَّمۡعِ ؕ فَمَنۡ یَّسۡتَمِعِ الۡاٰنَ یَجِدۡ لَهٗ شِهَابًا رَّصَدًا ۙ﴿۹﴾

"We (the Jinns) have sought to reach the skies but found it filled with stern guards and flaming fires. Indeed, we used to take up positions there to sit and eavesdrop. Now whoever eavesdrops will find a flaming fire waiting in ambush (to attack) him." (72:8 -9)

Prior to the revelation given to the holy Prophet ﷺ, the Jinns would go to the first heavens and secretly overhear and listen in to the conversations that would take place about future events. However, when the revelation commenced and began to be received by the Prophet ﷺ, the Jinns were prevented from reaching this point and when they would attempt to get close, they would find firm and watchful guards in position and balls of fire which would pursue them.

In the beginning, although the Jinns did have limited access to the first heavens to eavesdrop on the conversation of the angels but when the holy Prophet ﷺ received divine revelation, all the doors to the heavens were shut. The Jinns realised that something great was happening on earth. This caused the Jinns to disperse themselves throughout the earth in search for the new events that were unfolding on the earth, and it was there that a group of Jinns came across the recital of the holy Qur'ān by the holy Prophet ﷺ which caused the Jinns to submit and become believers.

وَأَنَّا لَا نَدْرِيٓ أَشَرٌّ أُرِيدَ بِمَن فِي الْأَرْضِ أَمْ أَرَادَ بِهِمْ رَبُّهُمْ رَشَدًا ۞

"We have no idea whether evil is intended for those on earth or whether their Lord intends guidance for them." (72:10)

The Jinns spoke about the fact that they did not know whether evil was intended for those who opposed the Prophet or whether they would end up following the Prophet, thereby being guided.

وَأَنَّا مِنَّا الصَّالِحُونَ وَمِنَّا دُونَ ذَٰلِكَ ۖ كُنَّا طَرَائِقَ قِدَدًا ۞

"Among us there are the righteous ones and those who are otherwise. We were of different ways." (72:11)

Similar to humans, the Jinns also have various religions and follow different paths. There are those who believe in Allāh ﷻ and therefore, are on the right path, and there are those who follow ways of evil and hence remain misguided.

وَأَنَّا ظَنَنَّا أَن لَّن نُّعْجِزَ اللهَ فِي الْأَرْضِ وَلَن نُّعْجِزَهُ هَرَبًا ۞

"We know that we are unable to escape (the punishment of Allāh) on earth and we shall never be able to escape from Him by fleeing." (72:12)

After listening to the revelation that the holy Prophet ﷺ brought, the Jinns became conscious of the fact that they would have to face accountability one day and they would find no place to hide if they chose to disobey.

يَٰمَعْشَرَ الْجِنِّ وَالْإِنسِ إِنِ اسْتَطَعْتُمْ أَن تَنفُذُوا مِنْ أَقْطَارِ السَّمَاوَاتِ وَالْأَرْضِ فَانفُذُوا ۚ لَا تَنفُذُونَ إِلَّا بِسُلْطَانٍ ۞

"O assembly of Jinns and men! If you are able to transcend (pass) the limits of the heavens and the earth, then try to do so. You will be unable to transcend without the power." (55:33)

This is also referring to the coming of a time that not only the Jinn, but man would also develop the ability of flight aviation in having the ability to travel through the earth's airspace.

Dismay on the Day of Judgement

يَقُوْلُ الْإِنْسَانُ يَوْمَئِذٍ أَيْنَ الْمَفَرُّ ﴿١٠﴾ كَلَّا لَا وَزَرَ ﴿١١﴾ إِلَى رَبِّكَ يَوْمَئِذٍ الْمُسْتَقَرُّ ﴿١٢﴾ يُنَبَّؤُا الْإِنْسَانُ يَوْمَئِذٍ بِمَا قَدَّمَ وَأَخَّرَ ﴿١٣﴾

"Man will say on that day, 'Where is an escape?' No! There is definitely no place of safety (to escape). On this day, the only abode (place of safety) shall be towards your Lord. On that day man will be informed of whatever (actions) he had sent ahead and left behind." (75:10-13)

وَأَنَّا لَمَّا سَمِعْنَا الْهُدَى آمَنَّا بِهِ ۖ فَمَنْ يُؤْمِنْ بِرَبِّهِ فَلَا يَخَافُ بَخْسًا وَلَا رَهَقًا

"Verily when we heard the guidance, we believed in it. Whoever believes in his Lord has neither loss nor humiliation to fear." (72:13)

إِنَّ اللهَ لَا يَظْلِمُ مِثْقَالَ ذَرَّةٍ ۖ وَإِنْ تَكُ حَسَنَةً يُضَاعِفْهَا وَيُؤْتِ مِنْ لَدُنْهُ أَجْرًا عَظِيمًا

"Undoubtedly Allāh is not unjust even to the extent of an atom's weight. If it were a good act, He shall multiply it and grant a tremendous reward from His side." (4:40)

A person will never be punished for a wrong that they did not perpetrate nor will Allāh ﷻ decrease any of the reward they are entitled to, even to the extent of the weight of an atom. No injustice will be done and a person shall be rewarded or punished according to their level of deeds that they carried out.

Those who carried out good deeds will be rewarded with goodness and those who carried out evil will be rewarded with the like thereof. If a person carried out one good deed, not only will the person be rewarded, but will receive at least the like of ten good deeds. And whoever carried out an evil deed, then only one evil deed will be recorded for them. This is mentioned in the following hadīth:

إِنَّ اللهَ كَتَبَ الْحَسَنَاتِ وَالسَّيِّئَاتِ، ثُمَّ بَيَّنَ ذَلِكَ فَمَنْ هَمَّ بِحَسَنَةٍ فَلَمْ يَعْمَلْهَا كَتَبَهَا اللهُ لَهُ عِنْدَهُ حَسَنَةً كَامِلَةً، فَإِنْ هُوَ هَمَّ بِهَا فَعَمِلَهَا كَتَبَهَا اللهُ لَهُ عِنْدَهُ عَشْرَ حَسَنَاتٍ إِلَى سَبْعِمِائَةِ ضِعْفٍ إِلَى أَضْعَافٍ كَثِيرَةٍ، وَمَنْ هَمَّ بِسَيِّئَةٍ فَلَمْ يَعْمَلْهَا كَتَبَهَا اللهُ لَهُ عِنْدَهُ حَسَنَةً كَامِلَةً، فَإِنْ هُوَ هَمَّ بِهَا فَعَمِلَهَا كَتَبَهَا اللهُ لَهُ سَيِّئَةً وَاحِدَةً

"Verily Allāh ﷻ has recorded good and bad deeds and He made them clear. Whoever intends to perform a good deed and does not do it, then Allāh ﷻ will record it as a complete good deed. If he intends to do so and does it then Allāh ﷻ will record it as ten good deeds up to 700 times as much or even more. If he intends to do a bad deed and does not do it then Allāh ﷻ will record for him one complete good deed. If he does it then Allāh ﷻ will record for him a single bad deed." (Bukhārī)

In another verse Allāh ﷻ says:

فَمَنْ يَعْمَلْ مِثْقَالَ ذَرَّةٍ خَيْرًا يَرَهُ ۝ وَمَنْ يَعْمَلْ مِثْقَالَ ذَرَّةٍ شَرًّا يَرَهُ ۝

"Whoever does an atom's weight of good will see it and whoever does an atom's weight of evil will see it." (99: 7-8)

وَوُضِعَ الْكِتَابُ فَتَرَى الْمُجْرِمِينَ مُشْفِقِينَ مِمَّا فِيهِ وَيَقُولُونَ يُوَيْلَتَنَا مَالِ هٰذَا الْكِتَابِ لَا يُغَادِرُ صَغِيرَةً وَّلَا كَبِيرَةً إِلَّا أَحْصَاهَا ۚ وَوَجَدُوا مَا عَمِلُوا حَاضِرًا ۗ وَلَا يَظْلِمُ رَبُّكَ أَحَدًا ۞

"The book shall be placed (given to them) and you will see the sinners afraid of what is contained in them. They will say, 'We are destroyed! What is with this book that it does not leave anything small or large unrecorded?' They will find their actions present and your Lord shall not oppress anyone." (18:49)

وَأَنَّا مِنَّا الْمُسْلِمُونَ وَمِنَّا الْقَاسِطُونَ ۖ فَمَنْ أَسْلَمَ فَأُولٰئِكَ تَحَرَّوْا رَشَدًا ۞١٤ وَأَمَّا الْقَاسِطُونَ فَكَانُوا لِجَهَنَّمَ حَطَبًا ۞١٥

"Certainly, some of us (Jinns) are Muslims while some of us are oppressors (disbelievers). Those who accept Islām have surely sought the path of good. As for the oppressors (disbelievers) they shall be fuel for Jahannam." (72:14-15)

In another verse Allāh ﷻ says:

يَا أَيُّهَا الَّذِينَ آمَنُوا قُوا أَنْفُسَكُمْ وَأَهْلِيكُمْ نَارًا وَقُودُهَا النَّاسُ وَالْحِجَارَةُ عَلَيْهَا مَلَائِكَةٌ غِلَاظٌ شِدَادٌ لَّا يَعْصُونَ اللهَ مَا أَمَرَهُمْ وَيَفْعَلُونَ مَا يُؤْمَرُونَ ۞

"O you who have īmān. Save yourselves and your families from the Fire (of Jahannam), the fuel of which is people and stones. Harsh and strong angels are appointed over it who never disobey what Allāh commands them and who carry out exactly what they are instructed (to do)." (66:6)

Conversely, a person who obeys Allāh ﷻ will be blessed in this world as well as the Hereafter. Allāh ﷻ says:

وَيَٰقَوۡمِ ٱسۡتَغۡفِرُوا۟ رَبَّكُمۡ ثُمَّ تُوبُوٓا۟ إِلَيۡهِ يُرۡسِلِ ٱلسَّمَآءَ عَلَيۡكُم مِّدۡرَارًا وَيَزِدۡكُمۡ قُوَّةً إِلَىٰ قُوَّتِكُمۡ وَلَا تَتَوَلَّوۡا۟ مُجۡرِمِينَ ۞

"O my people! Seek forgiveness from your Lord, then turn to Him (fulfil His commands). He will then send abundant rains to you and add strength to your strength. And do not turn away as wrongdoers." (11:52)

Water gives life to the barren earth. It is also used as a means of not only physical purification but as a spiritual purification.

وَمَنۡ أَعۡرَضَ عَن ذِكۡرِي فَإِنَّ لَهُۥ مَعِيشَةً ضَنكًا وَنَحۡشُرُهُۥ يَوۡمَ ٱلۡقِيَٰمَةِ أَعۡمَىٰ ۞

"Whoever turns away from My advice (the Qur'ān and dhikr) shall surely have a narrowed (difficult) life and We shall raise him blind on the Day of Judgement." (20:124)

When a person is afflicted with a trial or a tribulation and remains patient and engages in sabr (patience), then this will be a blessing from Allāh ﷻ. If on the other hand, a person is subjected to a calamity or an adversity and consistently complains and becomes despondent, then this is a sign that Allāh ﷻ is displeased with that person.

The predominant contributing factor which causes a person anxiety and depression is committing sin. This causes the heart to rust as mentioned in the following hadīth:

إِنَّ الْمُؤْمِنَ إِذَا أَذْنَبَ كَانَتْ نُكْتَةٌ سَوْدَاءُ فِي قَلْبِه فَإِنْ تَابَ وَنَزَعَ وَاسْتَغْفَرَ صُقِلَ قَلْبُهُ فَإِنْ

زَادَزَادَتْ فَذَلِكَ الرَّانُ الَّذِي ذَكَرَهُ اللهُ فِيْ كِتَابِه : كَلاَّ بَلْ رَانَ عَلَى قُلُوْبِهِمْ مَا كَانُوْا

يَكْسِبُوْنَ

"Verily, when a servant commits a sin a black mark appears on his heart. If he abandons the sin, seeks forgiveness and repents then his heart will be polished. If he returns to the sin, the blackness will be increased until it overcomes his heart. It is the covering that Allāh ﷻ has mentioned: No rather a covering is over their hearts from what they have earned."
(Ibn Mājah)

Allāh ﷻ says:

الَّذِيْنَ اٰمَنُوْا وَتَطْمَئِنُّ قُلُوْبُهُمْ بِذِكْرِ اللهِ ۗ أَلَا بِذِكْرِ اللهِ تَطْمَئِنُّ الْقُلُوْبُ ۞

"Those who have īmān and whose hearts are contented with the dhikr of Allāh. Behold! Hearts are contented with the dhikr of Allāh." (13:28)

Only through the remembrance of Allāh ﷻ will a person find true contentment. The emptiness and void that a person feels when they remain far away from the remembrance of Allāh ﷻ, very often is filled by many with drug and alcohol abuse; finding pleasure momentarily after taking it, before sinking back into the feeling of emptiness. The strength of the drug is commonly increased as the body becomes accustomed to the substance, until a person becomes heavily addicted and reliant upon these substances, which becomes a vicious circle in itself.

Those people who forgot Allāh ﷻ will be raised blind on the Day of Judgement.

قَالَ رَبِّ لِمَ حَشَرْتَنِيٓ أَعْمَىٰ وَقَدْ كُنْتُ بَصِيْرًا ﴿١٢٥﴾ قَالَ كَذٰلِكَ أَتَتْكَ اٰيٰتُنَا فَنَسِيْتَهَا ۚ وَكَذٰلِكَ الْيَوْمَ تُنْسَىٰ ﴿١٢٦﴾

"He will say, 'O my Lord! Why have you raised me blind when I was indeed one who could see?' He (Allāh) will say, 'This (is how it shall be for you). Our verses came to you, but you forgot them. In the same way you will be forgotten today.'" (20:125–126)

صُمٌّ بُكْمٌ عُمْيٌ فَهُمْ لَا يَرْجِعُوْنَ ۞

"Deaf, dumb and blind, they will never return (to the straight path)." (2:18)

وَأَنْ لَّوِ اسْتَقَامُوْا عَلَى الطَّرِيْقَةِ لَأَسْقَيْنَاهُمْ مَّآءً غَدَقًا ﴿١٦﴾ لِّنَفْتِنَهُمْ فِيْهِ ۚ وَمَنْ يُّعْرِضْ عَنْ ذِكْرِ رَبِّهٖ يَسْلُكْهُ عَذَابًا صَعَدًا ﴿١٧﴾

"If they remain steadfast upon the path, We shall definitely bless them with abundant showers to test them with it. Whoever turns away from the remembrance of his Lord, We shall enter him into a severe punishment." (72: 16:17)

Place of Prostration

وَأَنَّ الْمَسَاجِدَ لِلّٰهِ فَلَا تَدْعُوْا مَعَ اللّٰهِ أَحَدًا ۞

"Indeed, the masājid are only for Allāh, so do not supplicate to (worship) anyone else with Allāh." (72:18)

In this verse, the masājid refers to places of sajdah. It is not incumbent on a person to only prostrate in a masjid but any place which is free from impurity can also be used as a place of prostration. If a person is, for example travelling, so long as the place they are at is clean and pure, salāh in that place will be valid. The whole earth has been created as a purified place and a place of sajdah.

Intimidating the holy Prophet ﷺ

وَأَنَّهُ لَمَّا قَامَ عَبْدُ اللهِ يَدْعُوْهُ كَادُوْا يَكُوْنُوْنَ عَلَيْهِ لِبَدًا ۞

"When Allāh's slave stood up to supplicate to (worship) Him, they densely crowded around him." (72:19)

When the holy Prophet ﷺ would stand up for salāh, a few people would listen enthusiastically whilst the majority of the polytheists would gather around him as a way of intimidating him. They would encourage one another to make noise and clamour so that the holy Prophet ﷺ would become distracted and disturbed.

Throughout history, we find three different categories of people:

1. There are those that misinterpret Islām.
    Even though the polytheists knew that it was the truth, they refused to accept the message out of sheer pride and arrogance to the extent that they would boldly declare, "If this religion is the truth, then send stones from the heavens."

2. There are those that misunderstand Islām.
    Those who are misled and hence have a distorted understanding of the true teachings of Islam. During the time of the holy Prophet ﷺ, the Sahābah Kirām ؓ were the role models and represented the true teachings of Islām. If any misunderstanding arose, then even in visualising the behaviour of the Sahābah Kirām ؓ would be sufficient to rectify any misconception or confusion that arose, hence, Islām prospered when people took the Sahābah Kirām ؓ as their role models. The people entered into Islām in droves.

3. There are those who misrepresent Islām.
    There are many people who are Muslim by name but fail to practice their faith. Instead they practice such aspects which are distorted and alien to Islām.

قُلْ إِنَّمَآ أَدْعُوا۟ رَبِّى وَلَآ أُشْرِكُ بِهِۦٓ أَحَدًا ۝

"Say, 'I worship only my Lord and I do not ascribe any as His partner.'" (72:20)

After Allāh ﷻ, the status of the holy Prophet ﷺ comes next in rank.

Even though the Prophet's ﷺ status was so high, Allāh ﷻ states explicitly in the holy Qur'ān that he is still to be regarded as the servant of Allāh ﷻ. And this is a concept that He wished to distinctly clarify:

سُبْحَانَ الَّذِيٓ أَسْرٰى بِعَبْدِهٖ لَيْلًا مِّنَ الْمَسْجِدِ الْحَرَامِ إِلَى الْمَسْجِدِ الْأَقْصَا الَّذِيْ بَارَكْنَا حَوْلَهٗ لِنُرِيَهٗ مِنْ اٰيٰتِنَا ۚ إِنَّهٗ هُوَ السَّمِيْعُ الْبَصِيْرُ ۞

"Glory be to that Being Who transported His servant by night from Masjidul Harām to Masjidul Aqsā, the vicinity of which We have blessed, to show him Our signs. Undoubtedly, He is the All -Hearing, the All-Seeing." (17:1)

Even when Allāh ﷻ mentions the elevated status of the holy Prophet ﷺ to such an extent that he was blessed to be taken on the night journey, Allāh ﷻ still refers to the Prophet ﷺ as His servant. Allāh ﷻ could have used other words to describe the Prophet ﷺ such as the most beloved or the Messenger. This was intentionally inscribed to prevent any misunderstanding from arising, as occurred at the time of Sayyidunā Īsā عليه السلام. The people at the time elevated his position to such an extent that they ascribed him as being partners with Allāh ﷻ (by taking him to be the son of God).

The concept of tawḥīd had to be ingrained in the hearts of the people so that there was no room left for uncertainty or confusion. The concept of monotheism was set to prevail and every trace of idolatry had to be wiped away. Allāh ﷻ says in another verse:

إِنَّ اللَّهَ لَا يَغْفِرُ أَنْ يُشْرَكَ بِهِ وَيَغْفِرُ مَا دُونَ ذَلِكَ لِمَنْ يَشَاءُ ۚ وَمَنْ يُشْرِكْ بِاللَّهِ فَقَدِ افْتَرَى إِثْمًا عَظِيمًا ۝

"Verily Allāh does not forgive that shirk be committed, but may forgive all (sins) besides this for whom He wills. Whoever commits shirk has indeed invented a terrible sin." (4:48)

يَا أَهْلَ الْكِتَابِ لَا تَغْلُوا فِي دِينِكُمْ وَلَا تَقُولُوا عَلَى اللَّهِ إِلَّا الْحَقَّ ۚ إِنَّمَا الْمَسِيحُ عِيسَى ابْنُ مَرْيَمَ رَسُولُ اللَّهِ وَكَلِمَتُهُ أَلْقَاهَا إِلَى مَرْيَمَ وَرُوحٌ مِنْهُ ۖ فَآمِنُوا بِاللَّهِ وَرُسُلِهِ ۖ وَلَا تَقُولُوا ثَلَاثَةٌ ۚ انْتَهُوا خَيْرًا لَكُمْ ۚ إِنَّمَا اللَّهُ إِلَهٌ وَاحِدٌ ۖ سُبْحَانَهُ أَنْ يَكُونَ لَهُ وَلَدٌ ۘ لَهُ مَا فِي السَّمَاوَاتِ وَمَا فِي الْأَرْضِ ۗ وَكَفَى بِاللَّهِ وَكِيلًا ۝

"O people of the Book! Do not commit excesses in your religion and speak only the truth about Allāh. The Masīh Īsā, the son of Maryam was but the Messenger of Allāh, His Word that He cast (on) to Maryam and a spirit (soul) from Him. So, believe in Allāh and His messengers and do not say, 'Three'. It will be best for you to desist. Allāh is the only God. He is pure from having children. To Him belongs what is in the heavens and what is in the earth. Allāh is enough as a Defender." (4:171)

When the holy Prophet ﷺ would pray, the disbelievers would try to prevent the people from listening.

وَقَالَ الَّذِينَ كَفَرُوا لَا تَسْمَعُوا لِهَذَا الْقُرْآنِ وَالْغَوْا فِيهِ لَعَلَّكُمْ تَغْلِبُونَ ۝

"Those who disbelieve say (to each other), 'Do not listen to this

37

Qur'ān and make a noise (to disturb its recitation) so that you may be victorious.'" (41:26)

Abū Jahl, who was an arch enemy of Islām would encourage the people to disrupt the salāh by making a commotion, feeling afraid that people would accept the message if they had the chance to hear it because of its ability to penetrate the hearts. In fact, Abū Jahl himself, on a number of occasions, became so mesmerised and wonderstruck with the holy Qur'ān that he actually fell down into prostration when he heard the voice that commanded the people to fall down and prostrate.

Muhammad ibn Ishāq ﷺ mentioned that Az-Zuhrī ﷺ said that Abū Jahl, Abū Sufyān Sakhr ibn Harb and Akhnas ibn Sharīk once came to listen to the holy Qur'ān being recited at night, but these three men were not aware of the presence of each other. So they listened to the Prophet's recitation until the morning, and then left. They met each other on their way back and each one of them asked the others, "What brought you?" So they mentioned to each other the reason why they came. They vowed not to repeat this incident so that the young men of Quraysh would not hear of what they did and imitate them.

On the second night, each one of the three came back thinking that the other two would not come because of the vows they made to each other. In the morning, they again met each other on the way back and criticised each other, vowing not to repeat what they did.

On the third night, they again went to listen to the holy Prophet ﷺ and in the morning, they again vowed not to repeat this incident.

During that day, Akhnas ibn Sharik took his staff and went to Abū Sufyān ibn Harb in his house saying, "O Abū Hanzalah! What is your opinion concerning what you hear from Muhammad?" Abū Sufyān said, "O Abū Tha'labah! By Allāh, I have heard some things that I recognise and know the implications. I also heard some things whose meanings and implications were unknown to me." Akhnas said, "And I am the same. By Him Whom you swore by!" Akhnas left Abū Sufyān and went to Abū Jahl and asked him, "O Abul Hakam! What is your opinion about what you heard from Muhammad." Abū Jahl said, "We competed with Banī Abd Manāf (the holy Prophet 's ﷺ subtribe) and we fed as they fed and gave away as they gave away. So, when we were neck and neck with them, just as two horses in a race they said, 'There is a Prophet from among us, to whom revelation from the heaven comes.' So how can we ever beat them at that? By Allāh, we will never believe in him or accept what he says." This is when Akhnas left Abū Jahl and went away.

Everything is in the Hands of Allāh ﷻ

قُلْ إِنِّى لَا أَمْلِكُ لَكُمْ ضَرًّا وَّلَا رَشَدًا ۞

"Indeed, I have no power to do you any harm nor any good." (72:21)

The holy Prophet 🕮 had no supernatural ability or power and this concept of attributing any power to other than Allāh 🕮 had to be rooted out from their minds.

قُلْ إِنِّي لَنْ يُّجِيْرَنِيْ مِنَ اللّٰهِ أَحَدٌ وَّلَنْ أَجِدَ مِنْ دُوْنِهٖ مُلْتَحَدًا ۞

"Say, 'Without doubt, none can ever protect me from Allāh and I cannot find any refuge besides Him.'" (72:22)

If the holy Prophet 🕮 was to disobey Allāh 🕮 then he too would be subjected to Allāh's 🕮 wrath and anger. So the holy Prophet 🕮 would seek protection and refuge in Allāh 🕮 for He alone has the power to protect a person from all evil and harm.

إِلَّا بَلٰغًا مِّنَ اللّٰهِ وَرِسَالٰتِهٖ ۫ وَمَنْ يَّعْصِ اللّٰهَ وَرَسُوْلَهٗ فَإِنَّ لَهٗ نَارَ جَهَنَّمَ خَالِدِيْنَ فِيْهَا أَبَدًا ۞

"(My responsibility is nothing) Except conveying (messages) from Allāh and fulfilling His messages. (Thereafter) Whoever disobeys Allāh and His Messenger shall have the fire of Jahannam where they will live forever." (72:23)

The pronoun 'lahū' (لَهٗ) which is used in this verse refers to every person who will enter into the fire of Jahannam. This is used in a singular format. Then Allāh 🕮 mentions the Arabic word 'khālidīna' (خَالِدِيْنَ) which is plural. This is highlighting that every person who will enter the Fire of Jahannam will have a different level and degree of punishment according to the level of evil that they carried out. In terms of its structure, it will be specific according to a person's sin and for the disbelievers, this punishment will not cease and continue on for eternity. The Arabic word used in this verse for eternity is 'Abadā' (اَبَدًا).

There are three words which are interlinked:

- Abad (اَبَد) - it has no ending, as in the example of Jannah and Jahannam.
- Azal (اَزَل) - it has no beginning. Allāh ﷻ has no beginning as He has always existed.
- Sarmadī (سَرْمَدِیٔ) - it has no beginning or ending, for example Allāh ﷻ is Sarmadī.

Just as a person's status in Jahannam will be according to their level of deeds, similarly in Jannah, a person will also be rewarded according to their level of good deeds.

It is mentioned in a ḥadīth that the inhabitants of Jannah will be enjoying themselves, reclining on their couches when a particular person in Jannah will smell a beautiful fragrance. This person will ask Allāh ﷻ that up until this point, they had never smelt such a beautiful fragrance in their dominion before. Allāh ﷻ will then reply that the fragrance is coming from the Paradise above, and the only difference between them and that person above is that the other person had said one extra 'subḥān-Allāh' more than the person below.

Subhān-Allāh! How easy it is for us to do the dhikr of Allāh ﷻ now, which is light on the tongue and heavy on the scales, yet we are always preoccupied with worldly things which will bring us little benefit. The benefits of dhikr are mentioned in the following hadīth in highlighting its importance:

اَلطُّهُوْرُ شَطْرُ الْإِيْمَانِ وَالْحَمْدُ لِلّٰهِ تَمْلَأُ الْمِيْزَانَ وَسُبْحَانَ اللهِ وَالْحَمْدُ لِلّٰهِ تَمْلَآنِ أَوْ تَمْلَأُ مَا بَيْنَ السَّمَاءِ وَالْأَرْضِ وَالصَّلَاةُ نُوْرٌ وَالصَّدَقَةُ بُرْهَانٌ وَالصَّبْرُ ضِيَاءٌ وَالْقُرْآنُ حُجَّةٌ لَكَ أَوْ عَلَيْكَ كُلُّ النَّاسِ يَغْدُوْ فَبَائِعٌ نَفْسَه فَمُعْتِقُهَا أَوْ مُوْبِقُهَا

"Purification is half of faith. The phrase 'alhamdulillāh' (praise be to Allāh ﷻ*) fills the scale. The phrases 'subhan-Allāh' (high is Allāh* ﷻ *above every imperfection and need, and He is pure and perfect) and 'alhamdulillāh' together fill – or each fill –what is between the heavens and the earth. Prayer is a light. Charity is proof. Patience is brightness. The Qur'ān is either an argument for or against you. And everyone goes in the morning and sells himself, thereby setting himself free or destroying himself."* (Muslim)

Sayyidunā Abdullāh ibn Mas'ūd ؓ said that the Messenger of Allāh ﷺ said:*"I met Sayyidunā Ibrāhīm* عليه السلام *the night when I was taken on Mi'rāj (ascension to the heavens) and he told me: O Muhammad, convey my salām to your 'ummah and tell them that Jannah has good soil and sweet water but it is barren. The plantation of Jannah (is the recital) of 'subhān-Allāh', 'alhamdulillāh,' 'lā ilāha illallāh' and 'Allāhu akbar'."* (Tirmidhī)

Just as in the world we design our own houses and living quarters, in the same way we need to design our homes in Jannah, and this is only accomplished through the performance of dhikr and good deeds.

This is why Sayyidunā Alī ؓ would say "The world is going away from us and the Ākhirah is coming towards us. For every single one there are people. Be of those people who are from the Ākhirah and do not be from the people of the world. Now is the time to do practise, there is no accounts. Tomorrow there will be hisāb and there will be no time to do amal."

Allāh ﷻ says in the holy Qur'ān regarding those who follow His orders:

إِنَّ الَّذِيۡنَ اٰمَنُوۡا وَعَمِلُوا الصَّالِحَاتِ كَانَتۡ لَهُمۡ جَنّٰتُ الۡفِرۡدَوۡسِ نُزُلًا ﴿١٠٧﴾ خَالِدِيۡنَ فِيۡهَا لَا يَبۡغُوۡنَ عَنۡهَا حِوَلًا ﴿١٠٨﴾

"As for those who have īmān and who do good acts, Jannatul Firdaws (the highest levels of Jannah) shall definitely be their reception. They will live there forever and will never want to leave it." (18: 107-108)

When we imagine the concept of hospitality, we think of it as being for a small amount of time, for example as a guest. Therefore, the question arises that this hospitality may only be temporary. Immediately, Allāh ﷻ clarifies the perception that this will not be temporary but will be for eternity. Another question arises that something which is ongoing and eternal might get tedious and become boring, so Allāh 🕌 even answers this question in this verse by saying that a person will never get bored of Jannah because they will never want to depart from it.

The biggest treasure Allāh 🕌 has endowed us with is īmān. Even if we were to lose everything, if we have this firm and intact then every other adversity is bearable and of little consequence. This is our salvation on the Day of Judgement.

Some people adhere to a concept that no matter which religion you follow, the path it leads to is one. This is one of the greatest delusional misgivings a person can have and a product of Shaytān's handiwork. Our children are being taught concepts and ideas such as regardless of the religion they follow, they will all still end up in Paradise. As Muslims, we believe that Islām is the only religion acceptable in the court of Allāh 🕌.

إِنَّ الدِّينَ عِنْدَ اللهِ الْإِسْلَامُ ۗ وَمَا اخْتَلَفَ الَّذِينَ أُوتُوا الْكِتَابَ إِلَّا مِنْ بَعْدِ مَا جَاءَهُمُ الْعِلْمُ بَغْيًا بَيْنَهُمْ ۗ وَمَنْ يَّكْفُرْ بِآيْتِ اللهِ فَإِنَّ اللهَ سَرِيْعُ الْحِسَابِ ۞

"Definitely the only dīn (religion) with Allāh is Islām. Those who were given the book from before (the Jews and the Christians) differed only after the knowledge (of tawhīd) came to them because of hatred among themselves. Whoever disbelieves in the revelations of Allāh, verily Allāh is swift in taking account." (3:19)

Over the course of time and throughout history, many prophets were sent, but the message they proclaimed was one: to believe in the oneness of Allāh ﷻ and stay away from shirk and worshipping idols. When the message became distorted and adulterated, then Allāh ﷻ sent further prophets so that the truth could be propagated. This continued down the generations until Allāh ﷻ sent His last and final Messenger ﷺ and promised to protect His final revelation from any distortion or corruption.

In another verse Allāh ﷻ says:

وَمَن يَبْتَغِ غَيْرَ الْإِسْلَامِ دِينًا فَلَن يُقْبَلَ مِنْهُ وَهُوَ فِي الْآخِرَةِ مِنَ الْخَاسِرِينَ ۞

"Whoever seeks a dīn besides Islām, it shall never be accepted from him and he will be among the losers in the Ākhirah." (3:85)

Our Shaykh spoke of a dream that Shaykh Yūnus ﷫ once saw. He says: "I saw in my dream a person near my village whom I went to see. I thought to myself, 'This person has passed away.' This person used to believe that every religion was correct. I read two rak'āt of salāh and then said to him, 'Leave this ideology.' The person said, 'I will think about it.'" Shaykh Yūnus ﷫ could not help thinking why he had seen this dream because the person in the dream was no longer alive.

Thereupon the realisation dawned upon him that the person had children and the children may have continued to follow in his footsteps. When Shaykh Yūnus ﷫ woke up, he was weeping so profusely that all those around him began to weep too. He was reflecting on how difficult it was for the present generation to remain steadfast upon the dīn and was perturbed after reflecting on what would be the outcome of the future generations to come. Our pious predecessors had that fikr (anxiety) not only in seeking to purify their own hearts but also the betterment of society too.

Our Shaykh spoke about a house he had visited, which was a family of scholars but despite this, one of the siblings refused to accept Islām saying that he did not believe in anything. He would say to his other family members, "Have you seen anyone come back from the dead? So how can I believe in life after death?"

Man was created hasty and wishes for everything here and now. Many people may feel that because something is not visible to their eyes, then it cannot exist. Even if we analyse it through the lens of Science, we now know that many things exist which are not visible to the human eye. For example, microbes and viruses. Despite this, we know they exist because we feel their effects, for example when a person becomes ill. We also now have powerful microscopes through which these tiny microorganisms become visible to our eyes.

These minute particles may not be able to be seen but the detrimental effects of their presence are very real, to such an extent that these tiny organisms have the potential to cause a person to become severely ill or in the worst-case scenario, cause a person's life to end.

These living entities may be so miniscule that they seem insignificant in terms of their size, but the impact and effect they can have on a person's life are significant.

Only a few centuries prior, people were unaware that germs such as bacteria and viruses even existed and went about their lives without the slightest worry of taking any precautions and reducing the risk of being affected by their presence.

Just as we had the realisation that there are things that exist that we were not aware of, the question will naturally arise of how many more things might exist out there. Undoubtedly, there still remain a number of things that we are unable to make sense of, because of the limitations of our senses and intellect. There is a limit to the extent that our own reasoning and intellectual faculties can take us. To open the next set of doors we need to search elsewhere; from above and beyond, and this is where divine intervention in the form of revelation comes to our aid.

The common question that arises from those who are atheist and disbelieve is that if there is only one truth, then why are there so many religions, and because there are so many religions, how can we be certain that we are following the right one?

The simplest answer to this question is that we search for the one which can give us the best and most coherent explanation to the questions that we have just asked.

Islām explains the existence of all the other religions with the following explanation:

Since the creation of man, there has been the need for man to recognise as to why he even exists and hence find the purpose of his existence. For this, Allāh 🕌 sent prophets to various nations and tribes, guiding them to the worship of the oneness of Allāh 🕌 and teaching them that they would be accountable for their actions and deeds. Their life which they live in this world would determine what kind of life they would have in the next abode. This led to people accepting the message of the prophets and following them with the message they had been sent with.

Over time and through the course of generations, the truth of the message began to suffer from the effects of adulteration and corruption. Many practices that were alien to the teachings began to creep in. Those things that were permissible became forbidden and things which were forbidden became common practice.

Because of this reason, Allāh 🕌 would then continue sending one prophet after another in order to remind the people of the truth and abandon their misguided ways. This cycle continued and prophets were sent to instruct the people. The people would initially adhere to the message but then over the course of time, the message would become distorted.

All the other prophets were sent to a certain tribe or nation, but what is unique about the last Prophet to be sent was that his message was for entire mankind and was to be propagated until the end of time. Allāh 🕮 says in the holy Qur'ān that he would be sent as the seal of the prophets and hence would be the last and final Messenger.

Allāh 🕮 promised to protect His Book from any deviation and corruption. Those who would follow him would earn success and salvation, and those that chose to disobey would be doomed to an eternal life of damnation and misery.

What is unique to the holy Qur'ān that can be found in no other religion is that its Scripture has remained preserved in its original form. Not a single word has been altered or changed. The first original copy even exists in a museum today. And with scientific advancement, we now have the process of carbon-dating which can be used to validate its authenticity of being in its original state despite the passage of over 1400 years.

The exquisite eloquence of the holy Qur'ān comprises of a range of a stylistic and literary devices used throughout. It imparts deep wisdom and insight in order for us to live a life of virtue and uprightness. Also, there are facts and occurrences that are mentioned which have only either been discovered now or have occurred only recently. Alongside these aforementioned points, the detailed description given in the Qur'ān, further confirms and substantiates that this book could be from no other than the Lord of the Worlds.

Our Shaykh spoke about the lamentable plight of parents who would approach him after he had finished delivering a speech, and express their deep concern of their child or children having gone far away from the dīn.

One parent was speaking about his son, who although was studying his master's degree, had drifted so far from his religion that he felt it was irrelevant in this day and age.

The ultimate question which tends to be the defining line of whether a person accepts or rejects faith is the concept of justice. In this world, there are many people who seem to 'have it all' despite doing little to earn their income and position. In some cases, they may be the children of rich parents or have inherited a great amount of wealth after the passing of one of their family members.

On the other hand, there are others who despite toiling day and night; have little to feed their families. There are also those who commit horrendous crimes but are never caught, and others who despite living an upright life end up suffering great injustice and many a time, are wrongly convicted for crimes they did not commit.

As humans, we believe in the virtue of justice and we have a natural inclination and are predisposed to seek this out for the smooth and efficient running of our society, in order to prevent people from un-necessarily suffering distress and harm for crimes which they have not committed. We also have a natural affinity to help and assist those who are suffering. The suffering could be due to factors in a person's life which often are beyond their control and as a result they have undergone great difficulty. Then there are those who have led a luxurious life of existence although they have involved themselves in every single vice and wrongdoing.

Despite us human beings trying our level best, there always remains the possibility of arriving at a wrongful conviction. We come across many cases and examples where people are wrongfully convicted and are confined in prisons for years or even decades for crimes they did not even commit. Some even end up dying in prison only to be exonerated later. On the other extreme, there are those who walk away unpunished despite being involved in countless crimes and vices.

Just as our intuitive consciousness will not allow wrong to go unchecked without seeking a means of atonement or punishment, then this raises the question of what about all those wrongs that get overlooked or are out of bounds of being resolved because of the limitations of human ability and resources.

Those that lose their lives in war and famine; were they just created to be stricken with an ill-fated doom, to be eliminated and forgotten about like they had never even come into being? As humans, we believe that everyone has a right to existence and to live a peaceful and prosperous life, and this is what we try to achieve but for many, through no wrongdoing of their own, their life is cut short.

We may feel deeply saddened by these occurrences but aside from sympathising and consoling with those who have lost their loved ones in expressing and sharing the grief we may feel, there is little we can do to help these people or reverse the situation to any degree. But our intrinsic yearning compels us to have hoped to see these people be given the ability to live happy and fulfilled lives.

This intrinsic desire that we feel is innate in our nature and is to help us in understanding the reality of things around us. The worldly life remains unfinished and without closure there remains an element missing in our lives. We have been programmed to seek fulfilment and closure, and so the question naturally arises of whether closure will occur for those who were deprived of it in this world; who did not receive justice in this life. These questions naturally arise in a person's mind because of the intrinsic inclination within us for virtue and uprightness.

It is only through reflecting and contemplating on the holy Qur'ān that the answer to those questions which arise naturally are answered in providing the assurance of complete justice in the way which makes perfect sense and conforms to our own expectations that are innate within us – that goodness should go rewarded, evil and wickedness should be brought to account and dealt with accordingly.

The more virtuous and good a person is, the more they are deserving of a happier and prosperous life and similarly, the more evil and wicked a person is, the less they will be worthy of achieving success or prosperity because of the harm and suffering they inflict on others.

These questions are of the nature that only religion has the ability to answer and the best way to go about selecting the truth is by analysing the religion that complements our own nature, and has the ability to not only transform us into the best people that we can become, but the religion that makes the most sense and provides the greatest clarity. Undoubtedly, in light of all the scientific and modern-day discoveries that we have made, the holy Qur'ān is set apart from the rest of the religious Scriptures. Furthermore, it is the only Scripture that has stood the test of time and continues on giving and revealing its secrets as more discoveries are made and mankind moves into the future. If a person was to make a sincere study of it, then there can be no doubt left in a person's mind that this revelation is from none other than Allāh ﷻ.

A person wishing to seek and find the truth can achieve this by going back and re-examining the basic fundamental questions of life and existence. Then following it through with the natural affinity of their innate and intrinsic consciousness, alongside engaging in a serious study of the Qur'ān and analysing the information contained therein. This will, undoubtedly lead to the conclusion that these things could not have been known to someone living over 1400 years ago.

We are encouraged to feel that to be alive is a blessing and that we should try to cherish every moment of it, because it is brief and momentary and we do not know when it will end. To be alive and conscious is a gift. When we taste the gift of being alive and living, then the thought naturally arises that what if there was a way in which life could continue forever and that we could remain in existence and never have to be brought to an end?

The question of why no one has come back from the dead is because the time to be brought back has not approached and arrived yet. It will not come because we demand and expect it, but will arrive at its appointed time when Allāh ﷻ wills its coming. At that time, no one will be able to hold it back or hasten its coming.

The length of our own lives is significantly short compared to all the time that has passed since the universe came into being. But we as human beings in our arrogance want all miracles to take place here and now so that we can see them with our own eyes to believe it to be true. Yet Allāh ﷻ shows us the miracle of creation; the miracle of life, the miracle of nature's cycle in providing us with the nourishment that feeds and sustains our existence. He shows us the miracle of all the planets, the stars and all the celestial bodies that we see in existence. Despite all of this, we still fail to be moved.

In the same way, the people in the time of Fir'awn would say, "This is only mere magic!" Many today attribute this magnificent creation to be a form of 'magic' or some form of happening that randomly selected and organised itself in perfect harmony without the need of any help or intervention.

Despite being intelligent beings – many of us dedicate our entire life-time to the study of what we see around us and the way it functions, and yet we cannot master the complexity in the design and magnifi-cence in what we see around us, and then to think that this all arose from some unintelligent source – who are we really fooling and de-ceiving, if not ourselves?

With new discoveries being made in the field of DNA, there leaves no room to speculate that this could come about without meticulous planning. This led to famous advocates for atheism such as Antony Flew who had spent his entire life in disbelief, admitting to the fact that in light of the new evidence, he had come to the conclusion that left no room for doubt, there had to be a designer in the creation and structure of DNA and this could not have evolved by chance or mu-tation. This led to an outcry amongst the scientific community with many attempting to malign his character when he made his views public.

He said he would only go where the evidence led him to and after a lifetime of disbelief, he accepted that there had to be the existence of a being that brought all this into existence.

When a person accepts the existence of a supernatural creator, then the next step naturally is to analyse the different religions to see which one appeals most to a person. Antony Flew did not go on to accept Islām however, and the reason which he gave was as a result of his understanding of Islām which was understood through the media misconception and misinterpretation of Islām, which he held as a reflection of true Islām, as many unfortunately do.

Prophets that Were Sent

Approximately 124 thousand prophets were sent, of which, 25 are mentioned in the holy Qur'ān by name. In Sūrah An'ām, 18 of the prophets are mentioned in five consecutive verses:

وَتِلْكَ حُجَّتُنَا ٰاتَيْنٰهَا إِبْرَاهِيمَ عَلٰى قَوْمِهٖ ۚ نَرْفَعُ دَرَجَاتٍ مَّنْ نَّشَاءُ ۗ إِنَّ رَبَّكَ حَكِيمٌ عَلِيمٌ ﴿٨٣﴾ وَوَهَبْنَا لَهٗ إِسْحَاقَ وَيَعْقُوبَ ۚ كُلًّا هَدَيْنَا ۚ وَنُوحًا هَدَيْنَا مِنْ قَبْلُ ۖ وَمِنْ ذُرِّيَّتِهٖ دَاوٗدَ وَسُلَيْمَانَ وَأَيُّوبَ وَيُوسُفَ وَمُوسٰى وَهَارُونَ ۚ وَكَذٰلِكَ نَجْزِي الْمُحْسِنِينَ ﴿٨٤﴾ وَزَكَرِيَّا وَيَحْيٰى وَعِيسٰى وَإِلْيَاسَ ۖ كُلٌّ مِّنَ الصَّالِحِينَ ﴿٨٥﴾ وَإِسْمَاعِيلَ وَالْيَسَعَ وَيُونُسَ وَلُوطًا ۚ وَكُلًّا فَضَّلْنَا عَلَى الْعَالَمِينَ ﴿٨٦﴾

"This is Our argument that We gave to Ibrāhīm (to use) against his nation. We raise the stages of whoever We wish. Verily your Lord is the Wise, All-Knowing. We gifted him (Ibrāhīm) with a son (Ishāq) and (a grandson) Ya'qūb, both of whom We guided. We guided Nūh before (Ibrāhīm) and from his progeny (We guided) Dāwūd, Sulaimān, Ayyūb, Yūsuf, Mūsā and Hārūn. In this manner, We reward those who do good. And (We also guided and rewarded) Zakariyyā, Yahyā, Īsā and Ilyās, all of whom

were from the righteous. And (We also guided and rewarded) Ismā'īl, Yasa', Yūnus and Lūt. Each of them We favoured above the (people of the) universe." (6: 83-86)

After mentioning the 18 prophets, Allāh ﷻ says as a warning that even if they were to commit shirk, then all their good deeds would be rendered void and in vain:

ذَٰلِكَ هُدَى اللّٰهِ يَهْدِى بِهِ مَنْ يَشَآءُ مِنْ عِبَادِهِ ۚ وَلَوْ أَشْرَكُوا لَحَبِطَ عَنْهُمْ مَّا كَانُوا يَعْمَلُونَ ۞

"This is Allāh's guidance by which He guides whom He Wills from His bondsmen. If they commit shirk, then all their actions will be destroyed." (6:88)

حَتَّىٰ إِذَا رَأَوْا مَا يُوعَدُونَ فَسَيَعْلَمُونَ مَنْ أَضْعَفُ نَاصِرًا وَّأَقَلُّ عَدَدًا ۞

"Until they see what (punishment) they have been promised, then they will realise who had the weakest assistant and whose numbers were fewer." (72:24)

The disbelievers will be told on the Day of Judgement:

وَلَقَدْ جِئْتُمُونَا فُرَادَىٰ كَمَا خَلَقْنَاكُمْ أَوَّلَ مَرَّةٍ وَتَرَكْتُمْ مَّا خَوَّلْنَاكُمْ وَرَآءَ ظُهُورِكُمْ ۖ وَمَا نَرَىٰ مَعَكُمْ شُفَعَآءَكُمُ الَّذِينَ زَعَمْتُمْ أَنَّهُمْ فِيكُمْ شُرَكَٰٓؤُا ۚ لَقَدْ تَّقَطَّعَ بَيْنَكُمْ وَضَلَّ عَنكُم مَّا كُنتُمْ تَزْعُمُونَ ۞

"Undoubtedly you have come to Us alone as We created you the first time (birth) and you have left behind your backs (in the

world) what (bounties and luxuries) We had blessed you with. We do not see your intercessors whom you claimed had a share in you (in your worship). Indeed, your relations have been cut off and what you claimed has been lost to you." (6:94)

In the world, the disbelievers would ridicule and mock at the believers but the tables will be turned on that day, and the believers will emerge as the superior ones and will have other believers on their side, in interceding for them, whilst the disbelievers will have no protecting friend or helper. Even though the believers were perceived as being inferior by the disbelievers, but in the eyes of Allāh ﷻ, they are of a very high status.

Sayyidunā Abū Hurairah ؓ reported Allāh's Messenger ﷺ as saying:

رُبَّ أَشْعَثَ مَدْفُوعٍ بِالْأَبْوَابِ لَوْ أَقْسَمَ عَلَى اللهِ لَأَبَرَّهُ

"Many a people with dishevelled hair and covered with dust is turned away from the doors (where as he is held in such high esteem by Allāh ﷻ) that if he were to adjure in the name of Allāh ﷻ (about anything), Allāh ﷻ would fulfil that." (Muslim)

The disbelievers would ridicule and mock the believers as they passed by. This is mentioned in the following verse:

وَإِذَا مَرُّوا بِهِمْ يَتَغَامَزُونَ ﴿٣٠﴾ وَإِذَا انْقَلَبُوا إِلَى أَهْلِهِمُ انْقَلَبُوا فَكِهِينَ ﴿٣١﴾ وَإِذَا رَأَوْهُمْ قَالُوا إِنَّ هَٰؤُلَاءِ لَضَالُّونَ ﴿٣٢﴾

"When they (the believers) passed by them (the disbelievers), they used to wink at each other. When they (the disbelievers) returned to their families, they would return (still) mocking (the believers). When they (the disbelievers) saw them (the believers), they used to say, 'These people are certainly astray'." (83: 30-32)

Allāh ﷻ says:

فَالْيَوْمَ الَّذِيْنَ اٰمَنُوْا مِنَ الْكُفَّارِ يَضْحَكُوْنَ ﴿٣٤﴾ عَلَى الْأَرَآئِكِ يَنْظُرُوْنَ ﴿٣٥﴾ هَلْ ثُوِّبَ الْكُفَّارُ مَا كَانُوْا يَفْعَلُوْنَ ﴿٣٦﴾

"However, today (on the Day of Judgement) the believers shall laugh at the disbelievers while looking on from couches. The fact is that the disbelievers are being punished (on the Day of Judgement) only for what they did." (83: 34-36)

One of the Companions of the holy Prophet ﷺ was known as Julaybīb ◌. He was looked down upon by people because of his inferior status and his physical characteristics but when he died, the holy Prophet ﷺ buried him with his own blessed hands and referred to him as his beloved. It was only then, that many of the people realised that he had an elevated status in the Ākhirah.

Once, a person came to Sayyidunā Alī ◌ and put forward four questions, one of which was, "What is close and what is closer?" Sayyidunā Alī ◌ answered by replying, "Close is the Day of Judgement but even more closer is your own death. As Allāh ﷻ says in the holy Qur'ān:

إِنَّهُمْ يَرَوْنَهُ بَعِيدًا ﴿٦﴾ وَّنَرَاهُ قَرِيبًا ﴿٧﴾

"Verily they see it as being far off but We see it being near-by." (70: 6-7)

قُلْ إِنْ أَدْرِيٓ أَقَرِيبٌ مَّا تُوعَدُونَ أَمْ يَجْعَلُ لَهُ رَبِّيٓ أَمَدًا ۞

"Say, 'I do not know whether what you have been promised is near or whether your Lord has specified a lengthy term for it." (72:25)

Once Sayyidunā Jibrīl عليه السلام came to the holy Prophet ﷺ to teach the people about the dīn and one of the questions he asked was:

فَأَخْبِرْنِي عَنِ السَّاعَةِ

"Tell me about the Hour (the coming of the Day of Judgement)?"

مَا الْمَسْئُولُ عَنْهَا بِأَعْلَمَ بِهَا مِنَ السَّائِلِ

The holy Prophet ﷺ replied, *"The one who is asked about it is no better informed than the inquirer."* (Nasa'i)

In another verse Allāh ﷻ says:

يَسْأَلُونَكَ عَنِ السَّاعَةِ أَيَّانَ مُرْسَاهَا ۖ قُلْ إِنَّمَا عِلْمُهَا عِنْدَ رَبِّيۖ لَا يُجَلِّيهَا لِوَقْتِهَا إِلَّا هُوَ

ثَقُلَتْ فِي السَّمَاوَاتِ وَالْأَرْضِ ۚ لَا تَأْتِيكُمْ إِلَّا بَغْتَةً ۗ يَسْأَلُونَكَ كَأَنَّكَ حَفِيٌّ عَنْهَا ۖ قُلْ إِنَّمَا عِلْمُهَا عِنْدَ اللهِ وَلَٰكِنَّ أَكْثَرَ النَّاسِ لَا يَعْلَمُونَ ۞

**"They ask you about Day of Judgement, 'When will it occur?'
Say, 'The knowledge of this is with my Lord. Only He will make
it appear on its time. It will be weighty on the heavens and the
earth and will appear suddenly.' They ask you as if you have perfect knowledge of it. Say, 'The knowledge of this is only with
Allāh, but most people do not know.'" (7:187)**

عَالِمُ الْغَيْبِ فَلَا يُظْهِرُ عَلَىٰ غَيْبِهِ أَحَدًا ۞

**"He is the Knower of the unseen and He has informed no one
about His unseen knowledge." (72:26)**

Allāh ﷻ alone is عَالِمُ الْغَيْبِ (Ālimul ghayb - the Knower of the
unseen). Allāh ﷻ gives عِلْمُ الْغَيْبِ (ilmul ghayb - knowledge of the
unseen) to whom He chooses of His prophets and messengers. Being Ālimul ghayb and having ilmul ghayb are two distinct qualities of
Allāh ﷻ alone.

Guarding the Revelation

إِلَّا مَنِ ارْتَضَىٰ مِنْ رَسُولٍ فَإِنَّهُ يَسْلُكُ مِنْ بَيْنِ يَدَيْهِ وَمِنْ خَلْفِهِ رَصَدًا ۞

"Except His selected Messenger. So, He has despatched guards

(angels) in front of him (the holy Prophet) (and behind him)." (72:27)

When Sayyidunā Jibrīl ﷺ brought down the revelation to the holy Prophet ﷺ, he was accompanied by other angels. It is mentioned that when Sūrah An'ām was revealed as a complete Sūrah to the holy Prophet ﷺ, 70,000 angels accompanied Sayyidunā Jibrīl ﷺ. These angels were sent as guards as a mark of protection so that the deliverance of the message was not intercepted by any means.

When revelation would normally descend, four angels would accompany Sayyidunā Jibrīl ﷺ but the sheer scale of this Sūrah and its status prompted a greater number of angels being sent in guarding its deliverance.

لِيَعْلَمَ أَن قَدْ أَبْلَغُوا رِسَالَاتِ رَبِّهِمْ وَأَحَاطَ بِمَا لَدَيْهِمْ وَأَحْصَى كُلَّ شَيْءٍ عَدَدًا ۞

"So that He may know that they have conveyed (to the Messenger) the messages of their Lord. He has knowledge of their conditions and He keeps meticulous count of everything." (72:28)

This refers to the holy Prophet ﷺ being informed that the message he had received was in its pure form, free from being tainted in any way.

قُل لَّا يَعْلَمُ مَن فِي السَّمَاوَاتِ وَالْأَرْضِ الْغَيْبَ إِلَّا اللهُ ۚ وَمَا يَشْعُرُونَ أَيَّانَ يُبْعَثُونَ ۞

"Say, 'None in the heavens and the earth has knowledge of the unseen but Allāh. They (the disbelievers) do not even know when they will be resurrected.'" (27:65)

The Arabic word which is used in this verse for the unseen is اَلْغَيْب (al-ghayb). This word is prefixed with اَلِف لَام اِسْتِغْرَاق (alif-lām istighrāq). اَلِف لَام اِسْتِغْرَاق refers to the complete knowledge of the ghayb (unseen) and this is with Allāh ﷻ alone.

Some people refer to the holy Prophet ﷺ as knowing the ilmul ghayb (knowledge of the unseen), but this refers to the anbā'ul ghayb (news of the unseen) which was given by Allāh ﷻ.

When Muftī Shafī Sāhib ﷫ was asked the question, "Did the holy Prophet ﷺ possess ilmul ghayb?" He replied, "Yes. A tremendous amount."

This answer automatically rejected the knowledge of ilmul ghayb because there are no fractions in ilmul ghayb. When a person possesses ilmul ghayb there is no limit or no portions in it. Hence, whatever Allāh ﷻ chose to reveal to the holy Prophet ﷺ was through the knowledge He gave him. So therefore, it was anbā'ul ghayb (news of the unseen) and not ilmul ghayb (knowledge of the unseen).

Once the holy Prophet ﷺ stood on the pulpit after Fajr salāh and narrated everything that would take place up until the Day of Judgement. He did the same after the Zuhr salāh and also after all the other salāhs for a full period of 24 hours. One of the Sahābah mentioned that those who had good memories retained every piece of information, and those who did not possess as powerful a memory, retained as much knowledge as they were capable of.

Does this mean the holy Prophet ﷺ was Ālimul Ghayb (Knower of the Unseen)? Of course he was not. It was anbā'ul ghayb as he was given this information of the unseen which he was narrating.

Another incident relating to the knowledge of the unseen is the dream that Imām Mālik ؓ once had. Imām Mālik ؓ longed for death in Madīnah Munawwarah, and after he had performed his Hajj he would not leave Madīnah Munawwarah out of fear of death coming for him whilst he was visiting another place. Once he had a dream in which he saw the holy Prophet ﷺ and asked him, "O Messenger of Allāh ﷺ, can you tell me when I will die?" The holy Prophet ﷺ in response showed him five fingers.

When Imām Mālik ؓ woke up he felt confused. He thought to himself as to what the holy Prophet ﷺ meant by five? Was it five years, five months, five weeks, five days or five hours? He asked one of the mu'abbir (dream interpreter) for an interpretation of his dream. The mu'abbir said, "This does not refer to five years, five months, five days or five hours." He continued on in explaining that it referred to the following verse:

إِنَّ اللَّهَ عِنْدَهُ عِلْمُ السَّاعَةِ ۖ وَيُنَزِّلُ الْغَيْثَ ۖ وَيَعْلَمُ مَا فِي الْأَرْحَامِ ۖ وَمَا تَدْرِي نَفْسٌ مَّاذَا تَكْسِبُ غَدًا ۖ وَمَا تَدْرِي نَفْسٌ بِأَيِّ أَرْضٍ تَمُوتُ ۚ إِنَّ اللَّهَ عَلِيمٌ خَبِيرٌ ۞

"Verily the knowledge of (when) the Day of Judgement (will come) is only with Allāh. He sends the rains and knows (the details of) what is in the wombs. A soul does not know what it will earn tomorrow and neither does it know in which land it will

die. Undoubtedly Allāh is All-Knowing, Informed." (31:34)

وَعِندَهُ مَفَاتِحُ الْغَيْبِ لَا يَعْلَمُهَا إِلَّا هُوَ ۚ وَيَعْلَمُ مَا فِي الْبَرِّ وَالْبَحْرِ ۚ وَمَا تَسْقُطُ مِن وَرَقَةٍ إِلَّا يَعْلَمُهَا وَلَا حَبَّةٍ فِي ظُلُمَاتِ الْأَرْضِ وَلَا رَطْبٍ وَلَا يَابِسٍ إِلَّا فِي كِتَابٍ مُّبِينٍ ۞

"With Him are the keys (the knowledge) of the unseen, about
which none besides Him has any knowledge. He knows what is
on the land and within the oceans. He is (even) aware of every
leaf falling from a tree, every grain in the darkness of the earth
and every moist and dry thing is (recorded) in the clear
Book." (6:59)

This is to reinforce the concept that worship should be exclusively
for Allāh ﷻ alone and free from ascribing partners to Him.

In today's society, predominantly in the Asian subcontinent, many
people indulge in such practices that lead a person to shirk and kufr.
Many people go to graveyards and think that by calling upon the pious people who have died, that they will somehow be in a position
of interceding on their behalf and hence their du'ā will be answered.
Our Shaykh spoke of one such incident whilst he himself was visiting a graveyard and was doing ziyārah. Two youngsters who were
there suddenly fell into prostration at the graves. Shaykh immediately asked them as to what they were doing. One of the youngsters
gave back an expressionless stare at the Shaykh whilst the other
youngster took to his heels and ran away as fast as he could.

Shaykh could also hear some women folk who had gathered there at the graveside of the pious saints and were saying things such as, "Shāhjalāl Sāhib, grant me a child." This was referring to the pious person who was buried there. These people believed that by asking them, the pious dead people would intercede on their behalf with Allāh ﷻ and they would get what they wished for. They were not aware that this practice was blatant shirk.

Even to the extent that we cannot ask directly from the holy Prophet ﷺ when we make du'ā, we should ask from Allāh ﷻ alone.

Many of the pious people and saints were held in such high esteem to such an extent that even stories began to be fabricated about them. For example, a child had died and the mother had visited Shaykh Abdul Qādir Jīlānī ﷺ and requested him to bring her child back to life. The woman was unrelenting in her request and then Shaykh Abdul Qādir Jīlānī ﷺ accepted her plea. He went into Murāqabah (meditation) where he supposedly saw Sayyidunā Izrā'il ﷺ (the angel of death) who had a bag containing all the souls of the people who had died on that day. Shaykh Jīlānī ﷺ spoke to Sayyidunā Izrā'il ﷺ saying, "Take all the souls but give the soul of that child back because the mother is crying." Sayyidunā Izrā'il ﷺ then allegedly replied, "Allāh ﷻ has commanded me to take his soul so I have to do it." The story then continues on by saying that a scuffle took place and Shaykh Jīlānī ﷺ snatched the bag out of the hand of Sayyidunā Izrā'il ﷺ which resulted in all the souls coming out and hence all the people coming back to life. Sayyidunā Izrā'il ﷺ then went to Allāh ﷻ and was sobbing as he narrated what had happened to which Allāh ﷻ apparently said, "In front of Abdul Qādir Jīlānī even my orders are void!"

Na'ūdhubillāh! The great lengths the human mind is capable of concocting such fabrications is deplorable. This highlights the stronghold that Shaytān has on man in misguiding them despite constant reminders being sent of the truth.

And there are many who believe these stories without even questioning how such a story could be true, where a human is attributed to have a higher status than that of Allāh ﷻ! May Allāh ﷻ protect us all from falling into such vice!

In Islām, no intermediary is required as there is a direct connection between the slave and the master. Allāh ﷻ says in the holy Qur'ān:

وَإِذَا سَأَلَكَ عِبَادِي عَنِّي فَإِنِّي قَرِيبٌ ۖ أُجِيبُ دَعْوَةَ الدَّاعِ إِذَا دَعَانِ ۖ فَلْيَسْتَجِيبُوا لِي وَلْيُؤْمِنُوا بِي لَعَلَّهُمْ يَرْشُدُونَ ۞

"And when My bondsmen ask you about Me, verily I am close by (so call only on Me). I answer the prayer of the caller when he calls. So they should accept and believe in Me so that they remain on the right path (with valid beliefs)." (2:186)

In another verse Allāh ﷻ says:

يَا أَيُّهَا الَّذِينَ آمَنُوا آمِنُوا بِاللهِ وَرَسُولِهِ وَالْكِتَابِ الَّذِي نَزَّلَ عَلَى رَسُولِهِ وَالْكِتَابِ الَّذِي أَنْزَلَ

مِن قَبْلُ ۚ وَمَن يَكْفُرْ بِاللَّهِ وَمَلَٰٓئِكَتِهِ وَكُتُبِهِ وَرُسُلِهِ وَالْيَوْمِ الْأَخِرِ فَقَدْ ضَلَّ ضَلَٰلًا بَعِيدًا ۞

"O you who have īmān! Believe in Allāh, His Messenger, the Book (the Qur'ān) that He revealed to His Messenger and the Book (all the books) that was revealed before (to other messengers). Whoever disbelieves in Allāh, His angels, His books, His messengers and the Last Day, then he has indeed wondered far astray." (4:136)

This verse is referring to a person not only believing, but remaining steadfast upon belief.

It is narrated by Sayyidunā Abū Hurairah ؓ that the holy Prophet ﷺ said:

بَادِرُوْا بِالْأَعْمَالِ فِتَنًا كَقِطَعِ اللَّيْلِ الْمُظْلِمِ يُصْبِحُ الرَّجُلُ مُؤْمِنًا وَيُمْسِيْ كَافِرًا أَوْ يُمْسِيْ مُؤْمِنًا
وَيُصْبِحُ كَافِرًا يَبِيْعُ دِيْنَهُ بِعَرَضٍ مِنَ الدُّنْيَا

"Be prompt in doing good deeds (before you are overtaken) by turbulence which would be like a part of the dark night. During (that stormy period) a man would be a Muslim in the morning and an unbeliever in the evening or he would be a believer in the evening and an unbeliever in the morning and he would sell his faith for worldly goods." (Muslim)

May Allāh ﷻ safeguard us all from trials and tribulations and give us all the ability to be steadfast in holding fast and adhering to the dīn, Āmīn.

English Translation of

سورة الجن

Sūrah 72 Jinn
(The Jinn)
(Makki | 28 Verses)

Say, 'Revelation has come to me that a group of Jinn attentively listened to me (reciting the Qur'ān) and said (to their fellow Jinn when they returned to their places), 'Indeed we have heard a most astounding (wonderful) Qur'ān.'	1	قُلْ اُوْحِیَ اِلَیَّ اَنَّهُ اسْتَمَعَ نَفَرٌ مِّنَ الْجِنِّ فَقَالُوْۤا اِنَّا سَمِعْنَا قُرْاٰنًا عَجَبًا
It points towards righteousness so we believed in it and we shall never ascribe any partner to our Lord.	2	یَّهْدِیْۤ اِلَی الرُّشْدِ فَاٰمَنَّا بِه ۫ وَلَنْ نُّشْرِكَ بِرَبِّنَاۤ اَحَدًا
Most exalted is the majesty of our Lord, Who has neither taken a wife or a child.	3	وَّاَنَّهٗ تَعٰلٰی جَدُّ رَبِّنَا مَا اتَّخَذَ صَاحِبَةً وَّلَا وَلَدًا
Undoubtedly, the ignorant among us used to say things about Allāh that transgress the limit.	4	وَّاَنَّهٗ كَانَ یَقُوْلُ سَفِیْهُنَا عَلَی اللهِ شَطَطًا
And we always thought that no human or Jinn could ever lie about Allāh.	5	وَّاَنَّا ظَنَنَّاۤ اَنْ لَّنْ تَقُوْلَ الْاِنْسُ وَالْجِنُّ عَلَی اللهِ كَذِبًا

Indeed there were those from mankind who used to seek protection from men of the Jinns and (thereby) increased them (the Jinns) all the more in rebellion.	6	وَاَنَّهٗ كَانَ رِجَالٌ مِّنَ الْاِنْسِ يَعُوْذُوْنَ بِرِجَالٍ مِّنَ الْجِنِّ فَزَادُوْهُمْ رَهَقًا
They (these Jinns) thought as you (the sinners) think that Allāh shall not resurrect anyone.	7	وَاَنَّهُمْ ظَنُّوْا كَمَا ظَنَنْتُمْ اَنْ لَّنْ يَّبْعَثَ اللهُ اَحَدًا
We (the Jinns) have sought to reach the skies but found it filled with stern guards and flaming fires.	8	وَاَنَّا لَمَسْنَا السَّمَآءَ فَوَجَدْنٰهَا مُلِئَتْ حَرَسًا شَدِيْدًا وَّشُهُبًا
Indeed, we used to take up positions there to sit and eavesdrop. Now whoever eavesdrops will find a flaming fire waiting in ambush (to attack) him.	9	وَاَنَّا كُنَّا نَقْعُدُ مِنْهَا مَقَاعِدَ لِلسَّمْعِ فَمَنْ يَّسْتَمِعِ الْاٰنَ يَجِدْ لَهٗ شِهَابًا رَّصَدًا
We have no idea whether evil is intended for those on earth or whether their Lord intends guidance for them.	10	وَاَنَّا لَا نَدْرِيْٓ اَشَرٌّ اُرِيْدَ بِمَنْ فِى الْاَرْضِ اَمْ اَرَادَ بِهِمْ رَبُّهُمْ رَشَدًا

Among us there are the righteous ones and those who are otherwise. We were of different ways.	11	وَاَنَّا مِنَّا الصّٰلِحُوْنَ وَمِنَّا دُوْنَ ذٰلِكَ ۖ كُنَّا طَرَآئِقَ قِدَدًا
We know that we are unable to escape (the punishment of Allāh) on earth and we shall never be able to escape from Him by fleeing.	12	وَاَنَّا ظَنَنَّآ اَنْ لَّنْ نُّعْجِزَ اللّٰهَ فِى الْاَرْضِ وَلَنْ نُّعْجِزَهٗ هَرَبًا
Verily when we heard the guidance, we believed in it. Whoever believes in his Lord has neither loss nor humiliation to fear.	13	وَاَنَّا لَمَّا سَمِعْنَا الْهُدٰى اٰمَنَّا بِه ۖ فَمَنْ يُّؤْمِنْ بِرَبِّه فَلَا يَخَافُ بَخْسًا وَّلَا رَهَقًا
Certainly, some of us (Jinns) are Muslims while some of us are oppressors (disbelievers). Those who accept Islām have surely sought the path of good.	14	وَاَنَّا مِنَّا الْمُسْلِمُوْنَ وَمِنَّا الْقٰسِطُوْنَ ۖ فَمَنْ اَسْلَمَ فَاُولٰئِكَ تَحَرَّوْا رَشَدًا
As for the oppressors (disbelievers) they shall be fuel for Jahannam.	15	وَاَمَّا الْقٰسِطُوْنَ فَكَانُوْا لِجَهَنَّمَ حَطَبًا

If they remain steadfast upon the path, We shall definitely bless them with abundant showers	16	وَاَنْ لَّوِ اسْتَقَامُوْا عَلَى الطَّرِيْقَةِ لَاَسْقَيْنٰهُمْ مَّآءً غَدَقًا
...to test them with it. Whoever turns away from the remembrance of his Lord, We shall enter him into a severe punishment.	17	لِنَفْتِنَهُمْ فِيْهِ ۚ وَمَنْ يُّعْرِضْ عَنْ ذِكْرِ رَبِّهٖ يَسْلُكْهُ عَذَابًا صَعَدًا
Indeed, the masājid are only for Allāh, so do not supplicate to (worship) anyone else with Allāh.	18	وَاَنَّ الْمَسٰجِدَ لِلّٰهِ فَلَا تَدْعُوْا مَعَ اللّٰهِ اَحَدًا
When Allāh's slave stood up to supplicate to (worship) Him, they densely crowded around him.	19	وَاَنَّهٗ لَمَّا قَامَ عَبْدُ اللّٰهِ يَدْعُوْهُ كَادُوْا يَكُوْنُوْنَ عَلَيْهِ لِبَدًا
Say, 'I worship only my Lord and I do not ascribe any as His partner.'	20	قُلْ اِنَّمَآ اَدْعُوْا رَبِّيْ وَلَاۤ اُشْرِكُ بِهٖۤ اَحَدًا
Say, 'Indeed, I have no power to do you any harm nor any good.'	21	قُلْ اِنِّيْ لَاۤ اَمْلِكُ لَكُمْ ضَرًّا وَّلَا رَشَدًا

English	#	Arabic
Say, 'Without doubt, none can ever protect me from Allāh and I cannot find any refuge besides Him.'	22	قُلْ اِنِّیْ لَنْ يُّجِيْرَنِیْ مِنَ اللهِ اَحَدٌ وَّلَنْ اَجِدَ مِنْ دُوْنِهٖ مُلْتَحَدًا
(My responsibility is nothing) Except conveying (messages) from Allāh and fulfilling His messages. (Thereafter) Whoever disobeys Allāh and His Messenger shall have the fire of Jahannam where they will live forever.	23	اِلَّا بَلٰغًا مِّنَ اللهِ وَرِسٰلٰتِهٖ ۚ وَمَنْ يَّعْصِ اللهَ وَرَسُوْلَهٗ فَاِنَّ لَهٗ نَارَ جَهَنَّمَ خٰلِدِيْنَ فِيْهَاۤ اَبَدًا
Until they see what (punishment) they have been promised, then they will realise who had the weakest assistant and whose numbers were fewer.	24	حَتّٰۤى اِذَا رَاَوْا مَا يُوْعَدُوْنَ فَسَيَعْلَمُوْنَ مَنْ اَضْعَفُ نَاصِرًا وَّاَقَلُّ عَدَدًا
Say, 'I do not know whether what you have been promised is near or whether your Lord has specified a lengthy term for it.'	25	قُلْ اِنْ اَدْرِیْۤ اَقَرِيْبٌ مَّا تُوْعَدُوْنَ اَمْ يَجْعَلُ لَهٗ رَبِّیْۤ اَمَدًا
He is the Knower of the unseen and He has informed no one about His unseen knowledge.	26	عٰلِمُ الْغَيْبِ فَلَا يُظْهِرُ عَلٰى غَيْبِهٖۤ اَحَدًا

74

Except His selected Messenger. So, He has despatched guards (angels) in front of him (the holy Prophet) (and behind him).	27	اِلَّا مَنِ ارْتَضٰى مِنْ رَّسُوْلٍ فَاِنَّهٗ يَسْلُكُ مِنْ بَيْنِ يَدَيْهِ وَمِنْ خَلْفِهٖ رَصَدًا
So that He may know that they have conveyed (to the Messenger) the messages of their Lord. He has knowledge of their conditions and He keeps meticulous count of everything.	28	لِيَعْلَمَ اَنْ قَدْ اَبْلَغُوْا رِسٰلٰتِ رَبِّهِمْ وَاَحَاطَ بِمَا لَدَيْهِمْ وَاَحْصٰى كُلَّ شَيْءٍ عَدَدًا

Quranic Wonders

The science of Tafsīr in itself is very vast, hence the compilation of these specific verses provides the reader with a simple and brief commentary. It is aimed to equip the reader with a small glimpse of the profound beauty of the Holy Qur'ān so that they can gain the passion to study further in depth. It is hoped that this will become a means of encouragement to increase the zeal and enthusiasm to recite and inculcate the teachings of the Holy Qur'ān into our daily lives. **UK RRP:£5:00**

Protection in the Grave

Sūrah Al-Mulk encapsulates the purpose of our creation - that we were created to live a life of obedience to our Lord and Creator. This can only be made to manifest through our good deeds which we perform solely

for the sake of Allāh 🌟, in order to seek His pleasure. The Holy Prophet 🌺 told his Ummah to recite this Sūrah every night and learn this Sūrah by heart. The importance of this Sūrah is stressed due to the fact that the Holy Prophet 🌺 never slept until he had finished reciting this Sūrah. **UK RRP:£4:00**

Protection from Black Magic

These last ten Sūrahs are not only distinct in their meanings and message which will be discussed in this book, but also the fact that every Muslim should have these Sūrahs committed to memory as a minimum requirement in seeking refuge in Allāh 🌟 from all harm and evil, and every imperfection as well as seeking solace and peace in understanding His might and attributes. **UK RRP:£5:00**

Nurturing Children in Islam

Bringing up children has never been an easy duty. The challenges do not get easier as they get older either. Our emotions and other priorities sometimes hinder in nurturing our children, and as such, we fail to assist our children in reaching their potential by continually stumbling over our own perception of what we consider as ideal children. Our duty to our children is not without accountability. Our neglect and lack of interest in our children will be held to task. **UK RRP:£5:00**

Ready for Judgement Day?

For those that doubt the Day of Resurrection, Allāh ﷻ is reaffirming that there is no scope for uncertainty; this day is indisputable and will surely occur. The day when the truth will be laid out bare and everything will be exposed, there will be no place to flee or escape to. Regretting that day will be of no avail; excuses will fail to safeguard or shelter a person from breaking free and escaping judgement. **UK RRP:£4:00**

Flee Towards Allāh ﷻ

Sūrah Al-Ma'ārij begins by addressing the disbelievers who used to mock the Holy Prophet ﷺ about the Day of Judgement. In this Surah, Allāh ﷻ severely reproaches those who deny it assuming that there is only one life; the life of this world. The Sūrah manifests its horrors and catastrophic scenes that the entire creation shall witness on that very day. Mankind will then realise that on this horrific day, they will be judged by their own actions. **UK RRP:£4:00**

Lanterns of Knowledge

Once the commentary of Kitābul 'Ilm in Bukhāri was completed, we realised that this chapter is an entire topic in itself due to its fascinating and insightful perspective on knowledge. When compiling this commentary, there were many beautiful reminders as well as points of guidance for everyone's personal life as well as their lifelong quest for knowledge. Therefore, the commentary of this chapter alone would be beneficial for all seekers of knowledge and the idea of publishing it as a separate book came to mind. **UK RRP:£10:00**

TIME IS RUNNING OUT

As the title suggests, as each day passes, we come closer to our death. Life is too short to be treated as an amusement and for the fulfillment of one's lust. The Day of Judgement is inevitable where we all must one day stand in front of the Lord of the Worlds to give an account of our deeds. These six Sūrahs explain the horrors and terrifying moments of Judgement Day and the inevitable standing before the Lord. We must therefore prepare for the Hereafter by realizing our purpose in life; to worship Allāh ﷻ Alone and reduce our worldly expectations. **UK RRP:£4:00**

Best of Stories

Sūrah Yūsuf is more than just a story of one of our beloved Prophets ﷺ; there is much wisdom and lessons to be learnt and understood. All the knowledge comes from our honourable Shaykh, inspiration and Ustādh Shaykh Mufti Saiful Islām Sāhib. May Allāh ﷻ shower Mufti Sāhib with mercy and accept the day in, day out effort he carries out in the work of Dīn. **UK RRP:£4:00**

Call of Nuh

For 950 years, Sayyidunā Nūh ﷺ persevered night and day in continuous succession in preaching the message; unwavering and relentless in his mission. Not once did he feel that his calling was in vain. He stood firm and resolute in continuing with the mission that he was sent with, in proclaiming the message of the oneness of Allāh ﷻ; year after year, decade upon decade, century after century, but this failed to convince the people of the truth. **UK RRP:£4:00**

A Glimpse of Paradise

Time is the true wealth we have at our disposal though it cannot be amassed. The only way we can utilise it to our advantage is when we do righteous deeds and actions; for this will act in our favour in the Ākhirah (Hereafter). These moments will be preserved in exchange for moments of greater happiness and bliss in the next life. Therefore, we need to perform righteous deeds and actions in the short duration of time we have at our disposal in this temporary worldly life.

UK RRP:£4:00

Six Qualities of a Believer

Respected readers, do you want to be successful in this life and the Hereafter? The fact that you have prompted yourself to pick up this book and read, is an indication that the answer is *yes*. Or perhaps, you were not aware of the contents and purpose of this book and hence, eternal success wasn't the first thing on your mind. Nonetheless, it is easy to turn your attention towards this objective right now. **UK RRP:£2:00**

Living Islām in Modern Times

This book is a compilation of various articles written by Shaykh Dr. Rafāqat Rashīd Sāhib in the popular Al-Mu'min Magazine. Considering the great benefit these articles will bring to the Ummah, Mufti Saiful Islām Sāhib decided to edit and transform them into a book format, making the content easily accessible for readers.

UK RRP:£4:00

A CLEAR VICTORY

This book "A Clear Victory" is an enlightening commentary of Sūrah Al-Fath. It is cited in Sahīh Al-Bukhāri regarding the virtue of this Sūrah that Sayyidunā Umar Ibn Al-Khattāb ◉ reported that the Messenger of Allāh ◉ said: "This night a Sūrah was sent down to me that is more beloved to me than all what the sun shines over," then he read, "*We have indeed accorded a triumph to you, a manifest triumph, indeed*". **UK RRP:£5:00**